Gay SDAs: The Untold Stories

Juliana Harvard

Published by Juliana Harvard, 2022.

While every precaution has been taken in the preparation of this book, the publisher assumes no responsibility for errors or omissions, or for damages resulting from the use of the information contained herein.

GAY SDAS: THE UNTOLD STORIES

First edition. February 4, 2022.

ISBN: 979-8201037475

Written by Juliana Harvard.

Table of Contents

To SDA Kinship, who wants you to know that your story, your journey, and your life matter.

Preface

I am a Seventh-day Adventist and a lesbian—the first by choice, the latter by birth. I am not ashamed of nor apologetic for either aspect of who I am. Not anymore.

I spent well over two decades of my adult life not knowing, but always wondering, if there was anyone else in the world like me. I was a typical product of traditional Adventist heritage and culture, unquestionably assuming a belief that anyone who indulged in same-gender sexual activity would not enter the Holy City and eat from the Tree of Life. And yet, deep inside, I was well aware of the compelling strength of my desire to experience the forbidden pleasures I allowed in only my most secret fantasies. I knew that if I could "do it" for real just once before I died—as long as I didn't die *while* doing it—I could always ask God's forgiveness and still be saved and go to heaven.

Perhaps, I rationalized, by "doing it" I would "get over it." Perhaps the stark reality of experiencing fulfillment of my clandestine passion would be so utterly repulsive that I'd never even *think* about wanting "it" again. Or perhaps it was my God-given duty to fall into degradation—at least once—and then repent, so that I could effectively "minister" to others in my "condition." If only I could "do it"—just once in my lifetime.

Little did I know God would indeed call me to a *real* ministry for Adventist gays and lesbians—a ministry just as real as the Sabbath school teaching, the Pathfinder leadership, the homeschooling and health reform and musical services I provided for well over three decades within the Adventist congregations that I was always so much an active part of. But my present ministry bears no agenda other than showing and sharing God's unconditional love.

—*Juliana Harvard, Editor*

Introduction

By Ronald Peyton

My wife and I have often been asked how we can be gay-supportive when we are so firmly ensconced within heterosexuality. The answer lies in education. Specifically, it is the education obtained through association with those of whom we once had no knowledge other than the typical societal ignorance and misunderstanding.

As an Adventist pastor, I delivered typical Adventist sermons, citing homosexuality as one of the prime examples of the total depravity of society that showed we were living in the end times. I even quoted from the pulpit Pat Buchanan's hateful remark concerning the AIDS crisis: "The poor homosexuals. They challenged nature, and now nature is exacting an awful price."

By coming into contact with gays and lesbians during my ministry, both in evangelism and in visiting AIDS patients, I finally allowed the light to shine through and dispel the ignorance and darkness I had harbored. Another aspect of my path toward enlightenment was seeing the incredible hatred and insensitivity of church members. This was so out of harmony with the gospel message of Christ's love that we claimed to believe in.

Through the avenue of evangelism, one of the greatest educational experiences that I received in this area was meeting a lesbian couple, Dot and Barbara, and, through them, a gay male couple, Cliff and Gavin. Life is full of interesting twists and turns. While I thought I'd be educating them, little did I know I was the one who was about to receive the most important and life-changing education.

In 1983, I conducted a *Revelation Seminar* in San Antonio, Texas. The two women, Dot and Barbara, came faithfully to every meeting. Barbara was a retired Lieutenant Colonel from the U.S. Army. One day while I was visiting them, Barbara informed me that medical tests had confirmed a spot on her lung. This meant a terminal condition since the other lung had already been removed because of cancer. The doctor had given her less than six months to live.

In the *Revelation Seminar*, based on a literal application of Biblical texts, we covered the concept of building one's own "country home" in heaven. Dot told me how she and Barbara were sitting on their back porch one evening looking up at the stars and talked about how they looked forward to building their country home together up in heaven. Even in my naïveté and denseness I had figured out that they were lesbians. I couldn't understand why they spoke of being in heaven at all, much less together, since they were lesbians and obviously wouldn't find a place in the kingdom of God, anyway! Fortunately, I kept that piece of ignorance to myself and decided to simply minister to them and leave their case with God. I never encouraged or gave them an invitation to join the church. They began attending church faithfully, and I suppose we figured that was okay "as long as they weren't members."

I remember visiting Barbara in the hospital. Dot was at her bedside and pulled out a notebook to show me. It was a 24-hour chart, broken down into timed segments with friends assigned to sit with Barbara so she would never, ever be alone while in the hospital: 10–11am, Patricia; 11–noon, Sue; noon–2pm, Janet; 2–5pm, Jane, etc. And, when the time came for her to expire, she would not die alone. Such a display of love and devotion was phenomenal, rarely seen in heterosexual marriages, and certainly was not to be expected within some "perverted" arrangement. I questioned if such people were indeed so inherently evil, and whether they really were rejected by a holy God and would be denied entrance into heaven.

When Barbara died, I was asked to conduct the funeral. As a veteran, she was accorded full military honors. When the officer folded the flag, instead of following custom and giving it to her mother who was the next of kin, the officer handed it to Dot and then gave a crisp salute. I later found out that had been a request Barbara made sure would be honored at her funeral. Dot also informed me of another interesting request Barbara had made—she had requested that she be buried with no jewelry. I immediately knew the significance of that. Since Adventists have historically shunned jewelry, I suppose Barbara decided that if we would not invite her to join the church, then she was at least going to be buried looking like an Adventist!

Gavin, a friend from Alabama, had come to help Dot care for Barbara. Gavin was a dignified gentleman in his 70s, a "larger than life" type person who had such a quiet dignity and bearing that made you feel you were in the presence of someone special. He was like the dignified godfather of his circle. When Gavin spoke, people listened with respect, not wanting to miss even the nuance of his verbal nuggets.

At Barbara's funeral, Gavin introduced my wife and me to his husband, Cliff. We found out that a gay priest had secretly married Gavin and Cliff in 1946. They then introduced us to their 15-year-old daughter, Susan, who was Cliff's niece. When she was an infant, Susan's parents were in an automobile accident that killed her father and seriously injured her mother. Cliff and Gavin took Susan home to care for her while her mother recuperated in the hospital. When her mother was released from the hospital, she informed Cliff and Gavin that she did not feel that she could care for her daughter. So when Cliff and Gavin offered to adopt Susan, her mother agreed and signed adoption papers. Susan grew up calling Cliff "Daddy" and Gavin "Mama." She graduated from high school, got married, and within several years, made Cliff and Gavin proud grandparents.

Cliff and Gavin attended a local Baptist church. While the preacher was uncomfortable with them, he found it difficult and embarrassing to express his discomfort with them. When Cliff and Gavin cornered him one day and asked him precisely what the problem was, he stammered and finally said, "Y'all sing out of the same hymnal!"

During a revival, Susan responded to an altar call, which placed the preacher in a predicament. He refused to baptize her because her parents were two men, and at that point Cliff and Gavin decided it was time to move on and look for another church. They were willing to endure bias and discrimination and prejudice, but wanted to protect their daughter from suffering, especially when it came to where she was denied baptism.

They found a small Baptist church outside Mobile where the people accepted them, no questions asked. They were just looked upon as being two lifelong bachelors caring for each other and being so Christian as to raise their niece and provide a Christian home for her.

Several years ago, when I was serving as senior pastor for a local Adventist church, Cliff and Gavin came to visit us. At that time, we were trying to help a young church member come to terms with his sexuality without letting him feel threatened because we knew of his minority orientation. His family's social standing, background, and ethnicity all but demanded denial. Seeds of information could be planted that would make his dawning awareness a positive one when the time came for him to deal with such issues.

When we told the young man that Cliff and Gavin were coming to Chicago, he was extremely curious to meet these "two queers." When Cliff and Gavin arrived, we took them out for some of Chicago's famous deep-dish stuffed spinach pizza at Giordano's and invited the young church member to join us. He was excited! He had a friend from the academy who was spending the weekend, and he asked if he could come, too. We picked them up, and they piled into the backseat with Cliff and Gavin.

We later asked Cliff and Gavin if the young man came across to them as being gay. In typical southern manner, Cliff said, "Oh, Lawd, yes, tain't no question 'bout it." I asked him how he could tell, as the child appeared to be a normal child for his age with none of the obvious signs most people would look for, such as effeminate mannerisms. Cliff said something very profound and insightful that makes perfect sense. He said, "Aside from the obvious" (whatever he meant by that), "when them two boys climbed in the back seat, the straight one stuck his hands straight down in his pockets, but the gay one was very open and comfortable being on our laps. He was just more comfortable being close to another man—more so than the straight boy was." It was nothing sexual—just the unconscious comfortableness of the proximity, as though being physically close to another man was the most natural thing in the world. Through our socialization, Cliff and Gavin could help the young man without ever letting him feel threatened or know that "they knew."

Gavin once told a funny story of an encounter with an evangelist who had preached a revival series at their old church. The pastor, the one who had finally verbalized his problem with Cliff and Gavin as being "Y'all sing out of the same hymnal," decided he would invite an evangelist from Florida to preach a series on morality and the traditional family. Cliff, Gavin, and Susan faithfully attended each evening while this visiting evangelist railed against homosexuality as the "unspeakable sin" that is destroying the American family and bringing God's wrath down upon our nation.

One afternoon during the week of the revival, the pastor and evangelist paid a visit to Cliff and Gavin. It was a hot summer day, and Cliff was out mowing the lawn in loose shorts. When the pastor and evangelist arrived, Cliff came in and they visited in the kitchen around a long counter where they had bar stools. Because Cliff had been wearing loose shorts to mow the lawn, one of his testicles was half hanging out of the side of his pants.

As they were sitting at the counter sipping iced tea, and the pastor and evangelist kept trying to engage Cliff and Gavin in an argument concerning their personal living situation, Gavin noticed the evangelist kept looking down at Cliff's pants, leaning the bar stool he was sitting on further and further back for a better view. Finally, he leaned too far back and fell over, breaking the bar stool. He got up, embarrassed and apologizing, and Gavin looked directly at him. And right in front of the pastor Gavin said, "You wouldn'ta busted up our furniture if you hadn't been so intent on getting an eyeful of my hubby's nuts. I suggest you come to terms with your own self before you come here preachin' to us."

When Cliff and Gavin purchased their burial plots, Gavin asked the funeral director "which side is the wife buried on?" When the funeral director told him, "On the right side," he said, "That's where I'm to be." In September 1994, I received a call from Cliff that Gavin had died, just a few years shy of their 50th anniversary. Cliff asked if I could come down and assist their Baptist pastor in conducting the funeral. It was touching and heartening to see the love and support this Baptist church provided. Cliff and Gavin had finally found a church family that had accepted them fully and completely and did not question or pry into their personal lives.

As Cliff was shedding tears over Gavin's casket and wailing, "Oh, dear God, what am I gonna do?" one elderly lady came up and put her arm around him and said, "I know it hurts, Hon. I lost my husband two years ago, but he's in a better place now; and with time and the good Lord, it'll get better."

As an interesting aside, Gavin's last name was Lott. Trent Lott, the gay-bashing GOP majority leader senator from Alabama who curries favor with the religious right, is a distant relative of Gavin's.

To see Christians in a conservative religious culture from a southern town being so nonjudgmental and accepting of a gay couple was nothing less than mind-blowing. It shows that there is hope for people when they're willing to be educated. And, even if they remain uneducated and filled with misconceptions, they can at least be willing to reach out with love and compassion, regardless of their opinions; and let God be the sole judge.

My wife and I know several gay and lesbian individuals from a Seventh-day Adventist background and culture. We know many of those whose stories appear in this book. We hope these stories will help provide that education and enlightenment that many Seventh-day Adventists and other Christians need regarding God's gay children everywhere.

Ronald Peyton is a former Adventist pastor who lived in the Midwest.

Agape

By Juliana Harvard

I almost never left home before nine-thirty on a Sunday morning. But here it was, not yet eight o'clock, as I eased the front door shut behind me, careful to not wake my husband Denny and the two children who slept, blissfully oblivious to Mom's secret quest. On any other Sunday, I would have been rushing about inside the house, jingling keys and muttering to myself about what piano music I would need that morning to play at the Westside Methodist Church where I accompanied the choir and played hymns in between Sunday school and church service. This morning the sheet music was already in a flat black vinyl portfolio, sliding across the red leather of the passenger seat as I settled in behind the steering wheel. I released the handbrake and let the car roll backward down the steep driveway and onto the street before I started the engine. I was definitely not headed toward the Methodist church just a mile from our suburban tract home in west Fort Worth.

As my car crept up the entrance ramp to Interstate 20, an eight-lane thoroughfare quite unpopulated at this early hour, the warming May sun had not yet broken through an eerie gray dawn. An unseasonal chill swirled around my body in the unheated vehicle as I remembered the shock of first discovering the existence of an entire cyberspace community on *America Online* that I would have had only dared to imagine in my wildest fantasies. Denny had not been particularly amused to learn that his wife was interacting with Internet faggots and dykes, and he had threatened to disconnect the modem in the computer. So I logged on only in the late night hours, long after Denny and the kids were asleep.

I had been stunned but fascinated the first time I had seen "MCC" on the Internet, nearly five months ago now. "Metropolitan Community Church," explained the invisible voices behind the e-mail and computer bulletin board messages. The very idea of a church for homosexuals had seemed so incredulous, even when I finally located a Yellow Pages listing for a local congregation called Agape on the far east side of the city. *How could such deviants of society dare to pretend to worship God?*

With almost no traffic now, it was easy to spot the Anglin Drive exit. I clutched the wheel tighter as it began to slip in my clammy palms. My breath caught for a moment, suspended in eternity, as my pounding heart pushed hot blood into my cheeks. The first time I had pulled off the main highway onto that hidden access road behind the thick pink bricks that lined this part of the freeway, my best friend Megan had driven *her* car. It had been dark already that Saturday night when Megan and I were driving back from a Master Guide seminar in another Adventist church south of Fort Worth. Appealing to Megan's strong curiosity about the bizarre, I had convinced her to actually look for and find the Agape church.

Megan had been visibly nervous as she slowed down and turned furtively into the bumpy parking lot surrounding a modest brick building. "Welcome Home!" announced the plastic-lettered sign at the entrance. A half dozen strange-looking men stood near the door of the church. Seized by a paralyzing fear, Megan and I had both locked our car doors, and Megan drove quickly around the church and out the exit on the other side. Little did we realize then that, of all the places we could have been on a Saturday night in the Metroplex, this was one of the very safest for us. We hadn't known that the last Saturday night of the month was the Gay Men's Potluck at Agape MCC.

A few weeks after that Saturday night adventure with Megan, I had taken my son Adam to his algebra tutoring session on a Wednesday afternoon at the Hamilton Learning Center in east Fort Worth. Instead of waiting in the car for that hour as I usually did, I had decided to drive over to that clandestine place that Megan and I had so stealthily discovered under the cloak of darkness. I had had no idea what to expect in the daytime. Perhaps it would be like a Satanist church; after all, many of my church friends believed that homosexuality was a kind of demon possession.

The double glass doors of the church had been locked, but I saw a huge, soft woman sitting behind an old military surplus desk inside. She was big-boned and matronly, with very short salt-and-pepper hair and a warm smile as she unlocked one door from the inside. "I'm Jonee, Reverend Hunter's secretary.

What can I do for you?" she offered, smiling at me, a terrified suburban homemaker standing outside.

"Oh, well, I, er, just recently found out about your church here," I stammered. "I'd like to know more about, um, when your services are." Then I heard myself mumbling something about church music, whereupon Jonee brightened. "Oh, you'd love to meet our music director, Jonathan Eldrige. He's in the sanctuary now. Would you like to go in?" She started across the foyer, expecting me to follow, which I did. I wondered, "Could this motherly woman possibly be gay? She's assertive, but she's not brassy and crude as lesbians are."

The empty chancel was simply decorated, with bright cloth banners across the front and cloth wall hangings along the side, which I would learn later were panels for a very large quilt created as a memoriam for people who had died of AIDS. On one side of the rostrum stood a flagpole in a brass stand, from which hung a flag made of six colors in rainbow-color order from red to purple. On the other side, by the organ console, a clean-cut, obviously professional but very young man greeted Jonee.

"Jonathan, this is—" Jonee began, then turned to me. "I'm sorry, I didn't get your name."

"Oh, uh, Julie," I spoke quickly, caught off guard too fast to make up a name.

"Julie's interested in our music program here at Agape," Jonee told Jonathan. Then, to me, "I need to get back to the phone now. We'll see you later?"

I nodded politely, then turned back toward Jonathan. We talked easily and pleasantly. I learned Jonathan was a graduate music student at Texas Christian University in Fort Worth. He directed the Agape church choirs and handbell ringers, and occasionally even played the organ.

"Cindy would like to be able to pay an organist," he lamented. "But the church just can't do that yet."

"Who's Cindy?" I wondered aloud. Jonathan had referred in passing to his "spouse" without giving a name or gender.

"Oh, Reverend Cindy Hunter—she's the pastor of Agape," Jonathan informed me.

"Then who is your 'spouse'?" I asked next, hoping I didn't sound foolish.

"David Adams," he beamed. "He's also a music major at TCU."

"David and Jonathan!" I smiled wryly, thinking of the Bible story about the two young best friends, whose love for each other, according to the book of Second Kings, was "more wonderful than that of women."

Jonathan grinned proudly. "Yeah, it's kind of special!" Then, "You *must* come to our Good Friday service," he insisted. "We're performing the Fauré *Requiem* with the Agape chancel choir and a small orchestra that I've put together with student performers from the University. My conducting of it is my senior class project this semester."

"It sounds fabulous!" I truly wanted to attend. But in a *gay church*? How could I explain that to Denny and the kids?

That night, I had logged on to the internet as soon as Denny was asleep. "I'm thinking of attending a service at a local MCC. What should I wear?" I asked my faceless cyber-friends.

"It depends on the congregation," a lesbian from Utah wrote back, "but they're generally quite casual. I usually wear jeans, sometimes with boots, and a blazer. Let me know how you like the service!"

The combination of jeans and a blazer had been a new concept to me. In *church,* though? I knew I'd never be caught in anything other than high heels and a big-flowered print dress in the Methodist Church! But this was a concert, not "church" church, as I had known it all my life. Still, in compromise, I had worn a denim jumper and soft-knit collared shirt.

It had been easier than I had expected to casually tell Denny and the kids that I was going to a "boring" (to them) concert that Friday night in a "community church" on the other side of town. It had been dark, of course. No one had seemed to see me enter or leave. And, in comforting anonymity, I truly enjoyed the Fauré *Requiem.*

But today, this Sunday morning, was different. It was daytime again, and men and women stood outside the Agape church as I drove my car into the parking lot that was already nearly full. The women wore jeans and blazers and boots, and some were smoking cigarillos. The men, most of them slender and bald, waved graceful hands as they chattered, moving elegantly about the back patio. But all I could think was, "Yikes, there are *people* here! What if someone sees me?" I drove deliberately to the far end of the lot on the north side of the building, heading in toward a leaning eucalyptus tree that shaded a corner of the property and dangled its long leafy fingers lazily over the top of the car.

"Take it easy," I reprimanded myself, gently closing the car door as if to make sure no one would notice me.

I had already calculated that I could attend the MCC 9:00 a.m. worship service, leave at 10:00, and get back to Westside Methodist for their choir warm-up rehearsal at 10:30. Quietly, unobtrusively, I slipped into the sanctuary, sat on the side-aisle end of a back pew, and signed the attendance roster with the name of my Internet alter-ego Jewel Diamond. With my identity thus disguised, I could become part of the worship ritual, including taking of communion at the altar, being prayed for and served by gay men and women. The surroundings seemed no different from any of the mainstream churches that I had ever attended, except that the couples in the congregation were of the same gender. They sang the same hymns, except for using "inclusive language" that avoided the use of masculine and feminine pronouns and the use of gender-specific nouns like "lord," "king," and "father." I wasn't sure I could ever say The Lord's Prayer to "Our *Parent*, Who art in heaven." So far, no celestial lightning had struck me for blasphemy.

I listened warily to Rev. Cindy Hunter's sermon, as the round-faced woman with a fresh buzz cut, and obviously wearing jeans under her white clerical robe, spoke out against "The Lie" of fundamentalist Christian churches that God does not love gays and lesbians. For an agonizing moment, I want desperately to believe Cindy Hunter's words.

Then the service ended, as I expected, right at ten o'clock, leaving the necessary half-hour for me to drive across town to Westside Methodist. As I entered the glass-walled foyer, I was mildly dismayed to see that the menacing gray clouds had spilled large drops of water onto the warm asphalt outside. But as I approached my car in the parking lot, I suddenly was filled with helpless hysteria as I saw that the left rear tire was flat! "Oh, my God," I panicked, "what am I going to do?! I certainly can't call Denny—even if I could, I'd never get to Westside in time. I don't know anyone here. I can't ask any kind of favor from these...these total strangers."

Visions of unspeakable horror in untold dimensions filled my mind as I rushed back inside to find a phone—for what, I didn't know yet. I met Jonathan Eldrige in the foyer. He was the *only* person I knew or who knew me.

"Oh, Jonathan!" I gasped. "I have a flat tire, and I have to be at Westside Methodist in 30 minutes. Can I—is there a phone I can use?"

"Sure," said Jonathan, motioning for me to follow him to the reception desk where Jonee usually sat during the week. "Where's your car?"

"The burgundy '85 Dodge Lancer on the north side of the church," I said, unable to control my frenzy. "I don't know what to do!"

Numbly, my fingers dialed Megan's number. Megan lived only a few miles from here, but would she rescue me in my helpless plight? Megan, the good church lady, was not a morning person, and probably wasn't even awake yet.

"Okay, okay, calm down," Megan finally said, after listening with sleepy ears to me. "I'll try to get there."

"Well, you remember where the place is, don't you?"

"Yes, yes," Megan assured, with a yawn. "Don't worry." But even if Megan could take me to Westside on time, there would be the not-so-minor matter of going back to Agape MCC and getting the tire changed without Denny knowing about it. And how could I possibly drive Adam and Ashley to Debbie Basham's birthday party at 2:00 o'clock that afternoon at the Fort Worth Zoo?!

A quick flash of blinding lightening slashed through the glass doors of the church lobby, followed almost instantly by a deafening crack as thunder shook the frame of the brick structure. By now the rain was pouring down in sheets from the angry black sky. "I never should have come here today," I reproached myself, dropping the phone receiver in its cradle. "I know this is God's punishment for my sacrilege." I left the reception desk and started outside to wait for Megan when I heard my name.

"Juli," Jonathan called to me, "I asked David if he would change your tire. Is your jack in the trunk? Do you have a spare tire?"

Taken a bit by surprise, I said, "Oh—oh, thank you! Yes... yes, I think so."

Despite the torrential rain, David was already out by my car, surveying the situation. I rushed over to him, thanked him profusely, and unlocked the trunk. By now, a small crowd had gathered under the canvas shelter over the back porch to stare at this strange car, new to the Agape parking lot, as heavy water drops battered its metallic surface and bounced off furiously in all directions.

I turned at the sound of an amused chuckle coming from a big-breasted white-haired lady who stood arm in arm with another older woman whom I presumed was her domestic partner. "Well, well," the elderly lesbian chirped in her soft Texas drawl, "I never thought I'd ever see David Adams changing a tire!"

Indeed, David did not look comfortable with a tire iron in his hand, but he would do anything for his sweet Jonathan. As I watched, David was joined by an attractive woman named Ruth whom I had seen leading the dance liturgy during the service. Ruth *did* know what she was doing, and "helped" David change the tire, easily and quickly, even in the plain cotton button-front dress that she was wearing. Just as they were finishing, Megan drove into the parking lot.

I guessed correctly that Megan didn't really want to be seen here, and I rushed over to her car, explained briefly what had happened, and said we would talk later. Megan was fine with that and drove out of the parking lot as quickly as possible.

Then I turned to look at my on-the-spot benefactors, their clothes and hair dripping, soaked by the summer storm. Their genuine evidence of human love and compassion overwhelmed me. I hugged Jonathan, shook hands with David, and nodded and smiled at Ruth whose smooth, strong hands were covered with wheel grease. "I—I don't know what to say," I stuttered. "Thanks—thank you all so much!"

Across rain-slicked pavement at 45 mph on a wobbly spare tire, I rolled into the Westside Methodist parking lot just one minute before the choir was to process into the sanctuary singing the opening hymn. I had missed the warm-up rehearsal, but I was there to play for the service. I took a deep breath and sat down at the piano.

Soon the Westside Methodist choir, totally unaware of its significance in my quest, stood and sang the anthem for that day from the *Song of Isaiah*: "Surely it is God who saves me, I will trust in him and not be afraid, for the Lord is my stronghold and my sure defense, and he will be my Savior." A sparkle of light fused with color caught my vision, as sunlight peeked in suddenly through the amber and indigo pieces of the round stained glass window high above the south balcony. I sighed involuntarily, a long deep breath that shuddered somewhere deep inside me. Without a doubt, I knew it was okay with God that I was gay. *But would it be okay with the church? Only time could reveal what lay ahead.*

The rest of the day followed easily in its course. I told Denny that I had discovered the flat tire "in the parking lot of the church" and that "some church members" had changed it for me. I drove Ashley and Adam in Denny's truck to the zoo for Debbie's party, then came home and took the Dodge Lancer to Western Auto. Despite Denny's general annoyance at having to buy a new tire, I ignored his tirade. At long last, a rainbow had broken through the clouds.

Juliana Harvard writes first of coming to terms with God about her lesbian orientation. Her marriage, her children, her church, and her subsequent relationships are for later chapters.

Blame It on the Organ

By Michael LaCoste

I come from a good Adventist family. In fact, we were "seven-day" Adventists. Our religion governed everything we did not do. We ate no flesh foods. Tobacco, tea, coffee, and demon rum never touched our lips. Mother never wore a hat decorated with a feather. Dad never went to church without freshly polished shoes. How then did I come to direct my affections toward men instead of women? Could it have been that come sundown Friday dad did not throw the breaker on the fuse panel to cut off the electrical power? Did that lapse in righteousness by works vest the sins of my fathers in me?

Not that I was at all light in my sneakers. Throughout public grade school, I raced out to the playground with the rest of the boys at recess time, thrilled to have fifteen minutes to roughhouse, get a bloody nose and skinned knees. I loved playing soccer, football, and especially rugby where the object of the game was to grab the football and run with it until all the other boys piled on top of me in a satisfying tangle of sharp elbows, smelly feet, and panting chests.

Home was a mixed farm on the Canadian prairies where, along with my two brothers, I enjoyed the usual innocent little-boy pursuits. I poured pails of water down gopher burrows. I captured frogs and performed open heart surgery upon them after anesthetizing them with a rock. With my brothers and cousins, I played cowboys and Indians. In the winter, I built snow forts and started snowball wars. I enjoyed tobogganing and skating on the frozen river that ran through our property.

As I got older, I bumped across the summerfallow on the John Deere tractor, raising clouds of mosquitoes while cultivating the weeds into feigned oblivion. I drove the truck at harvest time, crank-started the gas engine that ran the auger, and shoveled grain without benefit of a dust mask. I milked cows, cleaned out the barn, flung dung upon the summerfallow, and heaved alfalfa bales into the loft. I helped dad fix fences, build bins, and pick potatoes. I was a normal, action-oriented farm boy that no one would have guessed was gay.

Well, I suppose there were a few clues. I took piano lessons and actually enjoyed practicing. I also enjoyed helping my daughterless mother with the housework; and since dad didn't quite trust me with the larger farm machinery, I was often lend-leased to mother while dad and my two brothers took care of the more complicated outdoor chores. Inside the house, I dusted the furniture, washed the dishes, made beds, scrubbed and waxed floors, and even learned how to whip up a cake from scratch. These enjoyable pursuits hinted at another side to my personality, and yet I might still have turned out to be most every woman's dream husband if dad hadn't sat down with *The Reader's Digest* one cold winter evening and ordered a multi-volume set of LPs entitled *Organ Memories*. I don't know what possessed him to order the album, a man who gained aural pleasures by tuning into the farm broadcast and *The Voice of Prophecy*. Perhaps he was hearkening back to the Friday evening vespers programs during his school days at an Adventist college. Whatever the reason, he wasn't too pleased with the album when it arrived, perhaps because it had one cut labeled *Wine, Women, and Song*. He quickly consigned the boxed set to a spot beneath a pile of *Western Producers* and *Country Guides*.

During one of my dusting forays, I discovered it and spirited it downstairs to my room where I loaded the LPs onto the RCA record changer. Before going to bed, I would switch it on and lie there in the dark, falling in love with Bach, Widor, E. Power Biggs, and Virgil Fox. This musical influence, combined with my entry into a composite high school populated by hundreds of beef-fed boys, may have been what tipped my personality toward the elfin side. I was soon in love with Mr. Barlow, my Grade 9 English teacher. How I resented his wife who each day drove up to the door in his new 1964 Pontiac Laurentian to pick him up for lunch. At night, as I lay listening to the pastoral tones of Bach's *Sheep May Safely Graze,* I imagined fiery accidents in which "that woman" would be fatally injured. I would rush to console Mr. Barlow, cradling his big shaggy head in my love-starved arms. I imagined myself sitting with my arm around his shoulders at the funeral, and since he was so paralyzed with grief that his very life was in danger, my dad insisted I move in with him to provide domestic care and comfort. After two hundred nights of such imaginings, you can picture my extreme disappointment when, towards the end of the term I brought my yearbook home and eagerly stood by as dad feigned interest in it. After glancing through the book he flipped back to my class picture, took off his glasses, peered closely at Mr. Barlow and said, "He's kind of a queer-looking fellow, isn't he?" I was speechless with hurt and disappointment. From then on, my imaginings involved *two* car accidents.

Despite these dreams, I never thought that my affectional orientation was warped. I assumed all males thought endearingly of the football and hockey players they idolized. Why else would my classmates spend hours watching *Hockey Night in Canada* where the players took delight in rolling around on top of each other on the ice? Why else would grown men attend games of the Canadian Football League to see beefy boys fondling each other's butts after well-executed plays? It was obvious that men loved loving men.

While all these thoughts were going through my mind, it was fortunate that my brand of Adventism prevented me from dating girls. I quite liked girls and I daresay I might have married one just to be like Mr. Barlow. Of course, I would never have dated a girl from school where the only Adventist female was my cousin. The other girls danced, watched movies in theaters, ate pork, and one or two even smoked cigarettes. There was no way I could have anything intimate to do with them. Sabbath School and church were peopled by more relatives, so there was nothing for it but to wait for college, not that I was looking forward to that. My parents, wanting to protect my older brother from worldly influences, had packed him off to one of our schools for Grade 11. There he had been promptly kicked out for improperly conducting himself in the company of girls, driving fast cars, drinking beer, and smoking. None of these delights appealed to me, so I attended a worldly college, but boarded with a very upright Christian couple who had come to Canada on Noah's ark and kept a close eye on my attachments, not that there were any attachments to monitor. I went to class each morning and came home every evening to do my homework, and that was the sum of my college life.

In fact, I had entered upon the frigid period of my life, which would last about ten years. After graduation, I began a successful teaching career in the big, wicked city, though the crime and dissolution had no effect upon me. My social life was confined to Sabbath dinner at the homes of several elderly spinsters who liked to look out for the young people. During the week, I spent most of my time outside the classroom preparing lessons to tickle the fancy of my fourth graders or taking extra courses at the university to upgrade my teaching license. My free time was spent reading wholesome books, in particular every book written about the Kennedy clan who had come to my notice one November Friday afternoon when the eldest son and his lovely wife visited Dallas, Texas. On my living room wall, I had a large poster of President Kennedy, and I kept a scrapbook filled with clippings reporting the family's activities. Perhaps it's not surprising that Bobby Kennedy was the first man to kiss me. In my dream, which remains vivid to this day, I was snuggled on his knee, comforting him about some mean thing Tricky Dick Nixon had said about him, and in gratitude he bent his head down and kissed me on the lips. This was while he was still alive, of course.

In the wicked city, I served as organist in the local conference's largest Adventist church. Early Sabbath morning I was downstairs playing the piano for the Junior and Cradle Roll Divisions. Then I would hurry upstairs and teach an adult Sabbath School class. I was at the organ for the church service and often back on the organ bench for the Adventist Youth meeting an hour before sundown.

I was a naïve young man, so I cannot remember when I realized I was gay, though it may have been after school let out for the term one June. Feeling liberated from the clamoring of my eager students, I was meandering through a bookstore when I discovered among the magazines one that showcased male models. The men weren't completely naked, but the towels they were coyly cuddling weren't exactly mammoth bathrobes. I was so startled that I bought the magazine along with a copy of *Playboy* to allay any suspicion the clerk might have had about my affectional orientation. Once home, I felt I owed it to myself to flip through *Playboy*, but the images disgusted me. Dad had been right. That sort of filth had no place in a Christian's home. I tossed it aside and concentrated on the male models in the other magazine. I told myself that I was just admiring them from a bodybuilding standpoint. I believed this rationalization because at the time I was a regular at a downtown gym, and the sight of those wholesome models with their muscular thighs and thick chests inspired me to work out harder.

Of course, I knew that looking at male models wasn't completely kosher either. I kept them at the bottom of my underwear drawer and sometimes even threw them down the garbage chute after a frightening sermon. However, in time, I would slip into the bookstore and buy some more. I was hooked on those glossy pseudo-friendships, which were both gratifying and totally unsatisfying at the same time. What I really wanted was a flesh and blood man to hold and cherish. Sitting in the choir loft during church services, I would study the men's faces in the congregation, willing just one of them to be my guy. My hopes ascended every time I saw a lone male walk in, but too often he was joined a few minutes later by a female who, through her body language, showed a close kinship with him. Was there no one in the Adventist church for me?

As one would expect, my first romance was brought about through my interest in the pipe organ, and I remember that cold November evening vividly. I walked over to a large United Church of Canada to attend their anniversary service, which included an organ recital. The organist had just begun to play when I was joined by Andrew, a practicing radiologist I had been introduced to at an earlier recital. It was good to see him again, and I moved over in the pew to make room for him to sit down. After greeting him, I closed my eyes to better concentrate on the music. After a few moments, I felt a knee against mine, so without opening my eyes I nudged myself over a little further in the pew; but, a moment later, his knee touched me again. *What was wrong with him?* I wondered. *Why did he keep invading my personal space?* I opened my eyes and looked at him. He smiled and winked. I smiled back, and in the exchange of glances I realized we were both special people. I snuggled over against him to enjoy the rest of the recital.

After the final hymn, we went to a coffee shop (hot chocolate for me, of course) and talked into the wee hours of the morning, exchanging life stories. Our romance continued with long Sabbath or Sunday afternoon walks and once-a-week excursions to a church for practice sessions where he was taking organ lessons. I would lie down on one of the pews in the choir loft while he practiced Bach's *Little Fugue in G Minor* and Clerambault's *Basse et Dessus de Trompette.* As I opened up to Andrew, I felt like a kernel of wheat that had been buried in the pyramids for centuries. Finally, I was alive. Finally, I had a friend with whom I could be real.

He wasn't an Adventist, but he was a Christian of the Baptist persuasion. He had heard of Adventists and knew a good bit about them, so I didn't have to explain about the Sabbath, coffee, and pork. I was thrilled that he was a radiologist because that would appeal to dad who had been disappointed when he could not afford medical school. I imagined him and Andrew having fascinating conversations about medical matters.

Coupled with my excitement at being in love was a fear that pursuing the romance would eventually result in my conversion into everlasting ashes. I studied the Biblical references that supposedly addressed our situation. The Jonathan and David friendship was promising but seemed a little weak since both boys were married, though they claimed that their love for each other surpassed love for a woman. I searched the public library and Christian bookstores for writings that provided prospects for special people like Andrew and me. Within their pages, I found a host of options: everything from lonely celibacy to marriage-like relationships that included sexual love. All the writers appealed to the Holy Scriptures to support their preferred options. Who was I to believe? I prayed that the Holy Spirit would guide me, but no particularly illuminating message came to me. Where was E. G. White's *Counsels to Gays and Lesbians* when I needed it?

During our walks, Andrew and I talked about these options. We knew that the Bible writers did not understand affectional orientation as it was now understood. Both of us were confident that we had made no deliberate decision to bend a naturally heterosexual orientation out of shape. Heterosexuality had never been our nature. So, presented with the truth of our affectional bent, we had to decide how best to live life to God's glory. Might it not be best to take St. Paul's advice and *marry* rather than go through life frustrated and lonely?

As I became more serious about the relationship, Andrew began pulling back. Finally, a few weeks after Christmas, he said that we should be friends, but not boyfriends. I felt like I'd been kicked in the stomach and promptly marched home and stepped onto the balcony of my 20th floor apartment, intending to jump. I had been disappointed in love and would quickly end the pain of my ruined dreams. However, it was January, and it was cold out there with a strong northwesterly whistling past the building; so I went back inside and went on with my life.

Going on was rather difficult. I couldn't walk past Andrew's apartment building, see cars similar to his, or hear certain organ compositions without thinking of him. There had been times before my friendship with Andrew when I'd been lonely, but now life was worse than lonely. Weekends were the worst. Saturday night the loneliness seeped out from beneath the fridge like dustballs and followed me around the empty apartment. My life wasn't made any easier by some women at church who felt it their Christian duty to commiserate about my single situation. After one of their more aggressive attacks, I decided I couldn't bear my burden of despair any longer. I would pour my hurt out at the feet of my parents. Aching with the pain of hiding my awful secret for so many years, I drove out to the farm and bawled out my disappointment over Andrew's rejection.

Mom and Dad had been hearing a lot about him during our courtship though I had not shared with them the exact nature of our attraction. Confronted with the reality of what he had long suspected, Dad put his arms around my shoulders and wept with me. Mother, who always looked at life practically, offered to heat some cinnamon buns and homemade soup. Both of them concluded that the failed romance was God's way of directing me away from an unnatural life. They wanted to help; and, in the first flush of parental concern, they snatched at whatever desperate measures they could invent. Dad wondered if papering my bedroom with centerfold pinups of naked women would help. Mother questioned whether marrying a lesbian might be an option. That way we could be a comfort to each other without having to bother about sexual relations. Best of all, no one would talk. Neither suggestion filled my heart with anticipation.

Back in the city I turned to the organ for comfort. Andrew had been practicing on a three-manual instrument. I would outdo him by finding the biggest organ in the city. This I did and engaged the organist for weekly lessons. The hours of practice filled some of the void, but I still yearned for someone male in my life. It was about this time that *The Council on Homosexuality and Religion* began telecasting a weekly half-hour show. The host interviewed various clergy, authors, and local personalities to show that gay people were not child-molesting monsters but contributing members of society like everyone else. After each telecast, the credits included a list of gay organizations. How surprised I was to see *SDA Kinship* listed in the credits one Sunday afternoon. I immediately contacted the show's host to ask for the address, and that's how I discovered that there were other gay Adventists. What a comfort it was to get in touch with several of them by mail and telephone. I was not alone.

I may have been a professional public school teacher, a well-liked Sabbath School teacher, and a faithful church musician, but I was terribly naïve about matters gay. I was thrilled with *Kinship* and the friendships I'd found there, but I lived in Canada and most of the Kinship members were in the United States. I was sure there must be some in my country and perhaps even in my province and city. I placed an ad for *Kinship* in the daily newspaper: *SDA Kinship, support for gay Adventists. Call 783-XYZX for information.* The telephone number I published was my own. A couple days later, the telephone rang. My ad had proved effective. Someone wanted to know more about *SDA Kinship*. And he lived right in my city. In fact, I knew him. He was the pastor of the church I attended! Not only did he want to know more about *Kinship*; he wanted to meet with me personally!

When I arrived at his office, he acknowledged my presence, invited me to sit down, and then continued typing some apparently urgent document. After about five minutes, he turned the electric typewriter off and swung his chair around so he was facing me. With no preliminaries, he asked whether I believed gay relationships were sanctioned by God. I said that I wasn't totally convinced but hazarded that from my study I thought God might meet gay people where they were just as he did Abraham who had taken two wives. God hadn't spewed him out of his mouth for doing that. And then there were David and Solomon with their hundreds of wives and concubines. I hypothesized that out-of-the-norm affectional partnerships may not be as big a thing to God as they are to humans.

He asked whether I believed God could change me. I testified I believed God could change me in any way he wished; however, despite years of prayer and study, it didn't seem that change of my affectional bent was in the works. I handed him a copy of *Kinship Connection,* which included the stories of several other gay Adventists who had prayed for change but had been disappointed. They had concluded that they must live the truth about their lives. Some of them recounted how God had led them to find Christian partners with whom they intended to share their whole lives.

The pastor didn't try to convince me that my conclusions were wrong. He simply opened the *Church Manual* and read a passage that indicated that living with another man would not be in keeping with church policy. He then explained that he didn't wish to expose me to the wrath of the church, so if I would write a letter asking that my name be removed from the church books the matter would go no further than a line item at an upcoming business meeting. I had invested a great deal in that church, practicing service music for hours each week, preparing Sabbath School lessons, and driving icy roads on Friday nights to get to choir practice. I refused to leave willingly. He then suggested that I ponder my position for a month, after which time a decision about my membership could be made. Meanwhile, I would have to relinquish my perch on the organ bench and in front of the Sabbath School class.

I didn't know how people would react the next Sabbath, but no one said anything to me as I sat out the program. Perhaps everyone was looking at me strangely and whispering behind their church bulletins; but, if they were, I was too naïve to notice. One lady sent me an *It Is Written* publication with a story about Colin Cook's *Quest Learning Center*. She wondered if his program might be of benefit to me. Pastor Cook's efforts were not news to me, for shortly after telling my parents about my affectional orientation they had sent me a large package of audio tapes published by his organization. I dutifully listened to them but couldn't make sense of them. If I remember correctly, his theory was that everyone is heterosexual though some may operate under the delusion that they are otherwise. If I kept telling myself that I was straight and acted upon that reality, I would be changed. (My parents read extensively and later came to the view that affectional orientation was genetic.)

The month the pastor had allotted passed quickly. I was busy with work and organ studies; however, I took the time to read over the "gay" texts once again. I realized the Sodom story was more about uncaring yuppies than men having sex with each other. Reviewing all the references to the story in the Bible, it was clear that both the men and women were bent on satisfying their own selfish lusts for wealth and a life of ease while they trampled upon the poor. St. Paul's references in Romans appeared to be linked to temple prostitution and worship of false gods. I could not see the link between any of the Bible references and my desire to love and be loved.

When the pastor called to ask for my decision, I could only say that my viewpoint had not changed. He sounded genuinely distressed as he told me that, considering my decision, he would be obliged to ask the church business meeting to discuss removing my name from the membership list. When he called a few days later to inform me that this had happened, he advised me to find a good man and settle down in a monogamous relationship. Meanwhile, he hoped I would continue to attend church.

I went for several weeks, but soon grew bored and began to stay at home on Sabbath mornings. I found an outlet for my musical gift in playing for Sunday-keeping churches. My search for a man continued; and, after a multitude of false starts, I found Mr. Alright. Shortly after we met, we moved west where we began attending church at one of the local Adventist congregations. My partner had never been baptized; and he was genuinely excited when the pastor, whom he admired, held an evangelistic series. At the end of the meetings, we were both thrilled when the pastor made an appointment to visit us. We were sure he would ask my partner if he'd like to be baptized. That Sunday morning we dusted the furniture, vacuumed the rugs, and even polished the mirror in the bathroom in case he would honor us by using the facilities. We set out our best mugs and a box of herbal tea along with a package of chocolate covered *Hobnobs* and then waited, and waited, and waited. We thought an emergency might have taken the pastor to the bedside of some dying saint. We expected he'd call later that evening to explain what happened. We dined. We washed the dishes. We watched the late news. We went to bed.

We were both disappointed, but we expected that there was a good explanation that would be provided when we saw the pastor on Sabbath. He greeted us warmly but didn't mention the planned visit. We continued to attend Sabbath School and church until one Sabbath when the lesson focused on witnessing. The teacher asked to whom we should direct our witness—one of those Adventist questions everyone knows the response to but no one wants to answer. After a silence, a very prim and proper sister spoke up, "Ellen White is quite clear that we should have nothing to do with homosexuals." Immediately, several people in the class disagreed with her; and before either of us could say anything, the discussion leader rushed on to other matters. Unfortunately, my partner heard nothing after the ignorant remark had been uttered; and from that day he refused to set foot inside the Seventh-day Prejudice church, as he christened it. I continued to attend for a few weeks, but then lost interest as well.

It was several years later that one member who had kept in touch called to say that the church had a new pastor who preached "nothing but Jesus." My partner was still locked in the ugly embrace of Miss Prim's ignorant remark; however, I decided to attend. The pastor upheld Christ in his sermons. After a few months, the church board asked me to assist with organ playing and teaching an adult Sabbath School class. I resisted both appointments, sure that eventually someone would make an issue of my affectional orientation and demand that I stop taking an active part in the life of the church. I clearly explained that, according to the *Church Manual*, I should not serve in either capacity since I was no longer a member. The elder asked if I'd like to become a member. I declined, remembering how a recent article in the *Adventist Review* had decreed that *"gay Christian"* was an oxymoron. How could I officially support an organization that sanctioned such an ignorant opinion that didn't even coincide with the *Church Manual's* admonition to love the sinner while hating the sin?

When the church board again requested use of my talents, I consulted one of my brothers who was employed by the denomination. He advised that gophers who do not wish to get shot keep their heads down. After further approaches by the church leaders, I agreed to help, which I continue to do today. Though the pastor is supportive, sometimes church members ignorantly and with some satisfaction condemn all homosexuals to hellfire. At times like that, I sense myself to be the queerest of all of God's creation: a creature trapped in a no-man's land between the hedonistic lifestyle of the world and the rigidly narrow prejudice of the church. As I leap and dodge from cover to cover in this no-man's land, I try to keep in mind that Jesus will be my ultimate judge and lawyer. Only He will pass judgement on whether I have clung to Him throughout this life or shunned Him. I am confident that He will save me, but I've asked Him to allot me a tiny cabin in heaven's back forty. I will be perfectly content to live quietly there with occasional visits from my Savior and Lord. The rest of the saints are welcome to the mansions.

Michael LaCoste (pseudonym), former public school teacher and public administrator, lives on Canada's west coast. He spends his days practicing the organ, freelance writing, and spreading the health message.

Castle's Kingdom

By Castledoll

"Fag!" they screamed at me. "Fag! Fag!" An innocent, confused seventh-grade boy, I ran to Mom as soon as I got home from school that day.

"Mom, what's a 'fag'?" I asked her.

"I don't know, Frank," she said, in throes of denial. After a long moment of silent recovery, she walked over to the bookcase and, with great ceremony, handed a dictionary to me, then sat on the sofa beside me.

My sweaty childish hands turned the pages awkwardly. What would I find in here? "F- fa- fag"—there it was. I read aloud, "A bundle of sticks to be burned."

Mom nodded, in relieved agreement. "Well, then, I guess that's what they were calling you." She shrugged, then rushed back to the kitchen to tend to the pot of potatoes cooking on the stove.

Slowly, I closed the dictionary, put it back into the bookcase, and headed for my room. I felt more confused than ever. The only "definition" of "fag" that was clear to me was that it was something not to be talked about.

I had been born the first child in my family, the first boy in our extended family. My grandparents were especially thrilled, since they had only two girls, my mother and my aunt. My stepfather, who raised me since I was five, was an only child and seemed delighted to have me for his son.

During my childhood, I had wanted to go to church and learn about God, but my family was not interested. All I knew about God was from watching Charlton Heston as Moses in the movie, *The Ten Commandments*. Then, when I was twelve, we moved next door to a Seventh-day Adventist family. They, of course, responded to my eagerness to learn. And I soaked it up!

I learned about the Sabbath, The Second Coming, and about pork and soybeans. I loved it! I was such a student of Daniel two and all the great

Bible prophecies. At my church, I felt accepted and loved. Adults would crowd around me after they learned that this 13-year-old boy was the only Adventist in his entire family!

But something else was happening inside me. I realized other boys were drooling over girls. I wasn't. I was dreaming of men. And now, at the tender age of 13, my classmates were calling me a fag.

In California where I was growing up, I heard about "it" constantly. Anita Bryant talked about it. Society hated gays. There was the Briggs Initiative (firing teachers because they were gay).

I read Bible verses about homosexuals. A Christian woman whom I looked up to told me that gays are reprobates, too far from God, and "He can't save them." I saw newscasts of gay pride parades and saw Christian holding up signs that said, "God hates fags."

I tried with all my heart to "be straight." I tried to drool over TV's "Charlie's Angels." I cried to God in my prayers, begging to become straight. Although my prayers to God took many forms over the years, the plea was always the same: "Make me straight like everyone else!" I felt so alone, and gradually my heart grew cold toward my Maker. How dare He make me gay!

At age 15, I left the church. I didn't give God any more time in my life. I didn't know Jesus; all I knew were the rules. Once I even attempted suicide; I had no hope. I felt damned just for being me. My teen years were hell. I didn't fit in anywhere. My home became terribly abusive. My once-beloved church wanted bright and shiny, straight people. Society treated gays like some sick joke. Where was I to go?

The Christian people didn't want me. Even the misfits of society think you're more of misfit if you're gay. There were no others like me. Where do I go to belong? Easy! The stoners! If you had a pipe and a bag, you were friends with them automatically. I needed desperately to "belong," so I belonged with a vengeance. I hung out with losers and became a loser. I did stupid things and got into trouble.

By the time I was twenty-one, I was addicted to gay porn but still very much in the closet in order to fit in with my stoner friends. They all had girlfriends, and I had to get one. I must not be found out! I tried to have a straight relationship, pretending I was straight, when what I wanted most was to be held and loved by a man! It was so unfair to my fiancée Chloe, and to our son Chip who was born outside of marriage.

One morning I was in a city bus accident in which one woman died. The rest of us who survived were not hurt. A lady sitting near me kept saying, "You never know when you might die. I'm so glad I'm saved. Better get saved!"

I knew very well what she meant, but I still thought God didn't—or couldn't—save me. I asked God, "Do You really want me?" A few months later, I heard His answer.

I had just come home from work when there was a knock at the door. An old man was giving out free books, so I took one, just because I love to read. I didn't look at the book until he had gone. Then I saw it was *The Great Controversy*! I knew it was an Adventist book, but I had never read it. In my amazement, I ran outside and caught up with the man.

"This is an Adventist book!" I exclaimed, breathless with excitement. "Are you an Adventist?"

The old man shook his head. He didn't seem to want to talk to me.

I turned back to my home and went inside. I opened the book to the last chapter. I read about the Judgment and how I would see my life as I had lived it and then see Jesus' life in a panoramic scene. I had to watch Jesus die for me, and it was too late because I was outside His kingdom. Oh, God, my Father, Lord, save me!

Right then, I knew He had saved me. Such a peace filled my whole being!

After that, I became a colporteur. I became a Sabbath school teacher for little kids. God blessed me. And then—I tried to have a girlfriend—again. (Oh, no, not again!) But, deep inside, I knew I was still gay. I couldn't share this shame with my lovely and faithful Body of Christ.

I became involved with ex-gay ministries, subscribing to "Love in Action" newsletters and "How to Be Straight" tapes from Colin Cook. This time I am a real Christian, and this time God will make me straight!

There is nothing like waking up in the morning believing by faith that God made you straight, and then finding you aren't. This went on for months and then years. It wore me out. My lust for men became stronger, and my faith in God became weaker.

I started going out to gay bars and getting into situations that I would have never dreamed possible. I became quite popular! I was the new attractive fresh face in town. The bar became a new family for me. Forget the church—I've found heaven on earth! But inside, I was empty, worse than ever before. I couldn't go back to God. I was gay, and no matter what I did, I couldn't change.

After several years, I began reading pro-gay Christian literature. Say what?! My mind couldn't wrap itself around this idea. I didn't know yet that I had godly people praying for me.

One night, after watching a video about God's love and awesome wisdom, and His control of universal events in this "great controversy," I sensed God was begging me to come back to Him. God wouldn't leave me alone! How can I come back? I loved sin. I loved my lover. I loved my Barbies. I loved my gayness. I had been out and proud for many years by now. I also had been in a serious, monogamous relationship with Bill for many years. Will all this perish when Jesus comes back?

Finally, I told God that I will choose to serve Him, but He will have to will that choice for me, because I cannot. I pray He will help me surrender all. I don't trust myself, but I'm still learning to trust Him and to believe that He really loves me and accepts me as I am.

I don't ask God to make me straight anymore. I can't fixate on that tired old concept! Many Christians still believe that God will make you straight when you turn to Him. I have found that not to be true in my case. Still, I will trust Him; He is so good to me. It's important to look at Jesus—not at others or at myself. There are so many things I don't understand, but I know God's promises are true. He is faithful!

The Psalms and Proverbs mean so much to me, especially reading in my favorite modern paraphrase, *The Clear Word*. Some of my favorite passages are Psalm 24:3, 4; Psalm 139; Proverbs 3:5-7; and Proverbs 24:16. I praise Him every day; if I don't, I will be overwhelmed by life's circumstances. But, when I fall, I get back up again. One of my heartfelt prayers to Him is for clean hands and a pure heart. Celibacy is a gift I'm learning to embrace.

Castledoll is a pseudonym.

Changes

By Peter Williams

PART I.

I have always had a homosexual orientation from a very young child. When I realized what it was called as a teenager, I would turn every shade of purple and red if I even heard the word *homosexual.* I was so ashamed of who I was; and, of course, like all teenagers of the '60s, dreaded that anyone should ever know I was queer.

I was raised in an SDA pastor's family and, in my late teens, abandoned all religion to do the typical "bad preacher's kid" things, such as smoking and dope. As a teenager, I was very withdrawn, mainly because of my orientation issues. I had very few friends except for the few older girls who mothered me in academy. I had a hard time relating to boys until I started doing dope, and then I was finally cool and accepted.

At about 17, I started trying to pick up older men by hanging around in public washrooms. I had two or three experiences that left me terrified and feeling guilty that I would get discovered. So I just buried myself in the dope scene and tried to stay away from sexual encounters.

When I turned 20 in 1971, I finally got up enough courage—once I had left home—to try sex again. I moved to Toronto to live with my grandparents and ended up becoming very involved in the scene. I was extremely active in it for about a year and a half.

When I was 22, I got scared of damnation (probably because of a bad acid flashback) and started going to church again. I quit drugs and sex and straightened my life out. In 1973, I headed off to Alberta and left my past behind for a new Christian life and an education. While at CUC, I met Jesus in a wonderful and new way after a very dark month of depression and near suicide. I quit smoking and was baptized about halfway through the school year. I was riding high on my newfound faith for the rest of the school year.

In the meantime, I met a wonderful woman who I fell for as a friend. We chummed around the entire school year and were inseparable. I had no intentions of ever marrying. For I knew I was gay, even though I had been converted. But somehow I thought God could change me. My friend and I got along so well that we ended up getting married in 1974.

We had a wonderful relationship in every way, and our relationship was especially deeply spiritual; the only area that was ever a problem was sex. I could make love to her, but it was like trying to push through a wall—kind of like when you try to push magnets with the same polarity together. I was still bothered by gay feelings but buried them deeply and never discussed them. I would perform my sexual duty and then try to run away for as long as I could before doing it again.

Soon I was getting even more deeply spiritual; and anyone from my church would say that I was the most wonderful spiritual Christian they ever knew. I actively supported the church in every way and even brought people into the fold by my wonderful witness. My marriage relationship grew, and we were very close in every way—except for the sexual area.

In the late 70s, I went through a major depression. I was incapable of holding down a job for about two years. I was an emotional basket case. I read the Bible constantly and read almost every E.G. White book ever published. I tried everything I could to get out of my depression. My wife would come home from work and I would literally be curled up in a ball on the floor, hugging a pillow, sobbing, crying, and groaning somewhere under the quilt over my head. I threw out everything from the house that had anything secular or pagan attached to it, like Christmas tree decorations, and classical music tapes with titles that might say something about wine or dancing.

The entire time I was wrestling with my "sinful" gay feelings and pleading with God to save me from this terrible demon which haunted me day and night. I grew out a beard so I wouldn't have to shave and look at myself in the mirror. I took very few baths and always with lots of bubbles, so I wouldn't see myself naked. I would go swimming—which I love—in remote lakes where I wouldn't see a man; and I would only swim with long shorts and a T-shirt. I don't think I saw my body for about two years.

I spent at least five or six hours a day reading the Bible and E.G. White, and the rest of the time praying for deliverance. I would go fasting for days; at one time was down to about 125 pounds, and I am 6 ft. 1 in.

In the summer of 1979, I went to BC [British Columbia] camp meeting and had about 17 demons cast out of me by a pastor and team who were into this ministry. It was so wrenching that I thought I would die. My tormented soul, however, found no rest; and I knew without a doubt I was damned. This horrible thought tormented me day and night. I was so tormented that I could barely even carry on a conversation. I was still gay but refused to accept it. I continued to cry day and night for deliverance from this for about three years. No one knew what the issue was.

In the early 80s, I finally adjusted to the constant wrenching psychic pain and forced myself to work again. I started accepting the fact that I was damned; but I got even more intensely involved in the SDA church to maybe prove to God I was okay after all.

In 1986, I was finishing up an apprenticeship as a funeral director and had to go to Vancouver to school for six weeks. I was absolutely terrified to go to a big city as I had literally holed up in a small, conservative farming community in interior BC for nine years. I wouldn't travel to any big cities, as they were surely too sinful.

My wife literally had to force me on the bus to go. Lo and behold, if I wasn't sitting next to a gay man the entire trip down! As I am a people person, I actually talked to him. I had a delightful conversation with him about his family and kids, and he told me how and why he had left his marriage.

Vancouver was a breath of fresh air. I got down there and realized it was a great city (I always was an urbanite). My spirit started to open up with the new experiences. By the time I got home, I knew I had to move out of that stagnant, stale, narrow town and widen my world. Within four months, we had moved to Vancouver.

I started to heal; one of the first things I did was look up a Christian support group for queers. It was a "change" type of ministry run by a former homo who was happily married, with children. I met some great guys, some of whom are still in touch with me. This is when I started to heal, for now finally the fact I was queer was "out" to me, anyway. Of course, I was working on changing it; at least I was talking about it and associating with other gay guys who had so much in common with me (we all wanted to change).

The year of 1986 was the turning point for me. This change ministry was indeed helping me heal. But it did not change that fact I was gay; it only helped me to admit it and bring it to the surface again, so I was no longer the emotional wreck I had been when I was burying it so deeply. I had finally come to accept the things I cannot change and had the wisdom to know the difference. I admitted to myself once again that I was indeed queer; and from then on, I started a slow healing process. The demons, at last, were losing their power.

The man who ran this ministry has, since that time, jumped back into the gay scene with a vengeance. He left behind a broken wife and children, for he is now dead from AIDS.

In late 1987, we moved to the Yukon. After about a year, I started attending The United Church, as the SDA church here was very cold and I did not fit in. I was too "gay acting" and from the big city. In 1990, I had my membership transferred to the United Church of Canada where I am still a member. Shortly after this, I became their organist. In the meantime, I was moving slowly to fully embrace myself as a gay man. Joining the United Church was a significant step in my self-acceptance, as they accept homosexuals, even in the ministry. Our current pastor (since 1993) is gay and in a monogamous relationship; so I feel safe and accepted in this church, and it is now my home. Remember, I am already one of the "damned" so it really doesn't matter that I go to church on Sunday.

I started to not only accept myself, but I realized the Creator had made me extremely creative and talented; perhaps being gay was just one of the added benefits of being a creative spirit. As I came to this deeper level of acceptance, I started to compose music. My creativity started to gush forth as never before. I was growing more comfortable with myself; and the more comfortable I became, the more creative I became. I realized I was caught up in a *true* change ministry, as I was slowly changing into a beautiful, creative, very sensitive and loving gay man. I started to like myself and started to thank the Creator for making me so unique. The more I grew to like myself, the more love I had to give others, and the more the music poured forth.

Do I believe in change? Absolutely! The Creator changed me from a wretched, damned, trembling, emotional wreck and has turned me into a loving, caring, accepting, creative, happy queer man. My heart is so full of gratitude and praise for delivering me from the demons that whispered to me that being homosexual was a sin, that my heart wants to explode; and I cannot help but pour forth in hymns of praise! I have written over 75 "church" hymns and songs. I had to force myself to stop for a bit as my hearing was suffering from having headphones on continually.

This is not the end of my journey. In the summer of 1998, I had some experiences on a two-week holiday in Toronto that allowed me finally to come out fully and completely here in my home community. This process is healed me at even a deeper level than I ever thought possible as I came to fully celebrate the wonderful gift and uniqueness of being queer. I love that Q word!

I discovered that, for me, the secret for genuine change and growth, and spiritual, emotional, and relationship healing, is simply coming out! It was the best, kindest, and most loving thing I have ever done for myself! How could it have taken me 47 years to finally get here? Behold all things are made new!

I am shouting from the mountains the good news—the Creator can change me from a codependent, clinging, insecure, fearful, self-hating child, to a fully mature, loving, centered and very-proud-to-be-gay man.

PART II.

Toronto was where I had lived in the early '70s and was very active in the gay scene. I had moved west in 1973 to attend school at CUC in Alberta. This is where I met the lovely woman who is now my wife, as I explained in Part I of my story. I had been back to Toronto only twice since the end of the 70's and had forgotten how much I loved that city.

I went down on a last-minute whim to meet my mom and sister who were traveling through there from Boston to see all the relatives in S. Ontario where most of my family lives; they were celebrating their 70th and 40th birthdays by visiting relatives. I thought I'd fly down to surprise them. I had a wonderful time drinking in the human beauty of this most multicultural city in the world. I love diversity with a passion!

From the minute I got off the plane and on to the subway, I knew I was home. I met so many wonderful people. I didn't realize until I got there that my spirit was so dried up that I had nothing more to give; and my thirsty soul drank deeply of the plethora of sight, sound, and cultures. The more my spirit drank, the more I could open myself to everyone I met. Being all alone, I had no one to relate to except the person sitting beside me on the streetcar or the squeegee kid standing on the corner waiting to wash car windows when the light turned red. I connected with the complete range of humanity—poets, philosophers, street kids, new immigrants, and—most wonderfully—gay men.

I was staying in the gay area of Toronto by choice, as I wanted to experience the community there. I did the family thing; when my mom and sister left to go back to Boston, I changed my ticket to stay longer, since I was having such a rich time there.

One day I was walking through a park in the gay ghetto, and I chanced upon the AIDS memorial in the park there. I was overcome with emotion as I stood there reading the names and wondering if any of those were men I had had sex with in the early '70s when I lived there. Suddenly I had this overwhelming feeling, like the Creator was standing next to me and saying, "Here you are today, a living, breathing man. Your name should have been up there, but I had work for you to do. Here you are today, a gifted composer, and alive; if you hadn't gotten married, you would have come back here and ended up in the gay scene again and today be up there as a name on a monument." I was overwhelmed.

About that time I was standing in front of that monument, my wife Erin, back home in Whitehorse, was writing me a letter. She read it to me that night on the phone when I called her.

In it, she told me something that she had never told me this before. A few months before she married me she had had a vision in which she saw a long black tunnel with a very faint glimmer of light at the end. She was told she had to go through it. It was revealed to her that the tunnel meant she must marry me (a gay man)—she knew I was gay. She was left crying prostrate on the floor and couldn't get up for two hours after this vision. She continued in her letter: "I know now I was sent to save your life, but now the tunnel is behind and I must let you go. It is safe now to let you go, and it is okay. Your life has been spared, and now you must make a choice and walk free." She was crying as she read it to me over the phone, and I was struck like a lightning bolt had hit me.

I always get cold feet before I leave on a trip, and I had wanted to cancel this one at the last minute. But Erin had told me before I left, "I don't know why I feel this way, but you *have* to go on this trip. There is a destiny in this trip for you and you will never be the same when you return." (She always has been one step ahead of me.)

That same night, I met Ross. This is how it happened.

I was standing outside the door of a bath house on Monday night, wondering if I should go in and look around for a while. (I liked to go look but did not have sex when I was in a bathhouse, as I respected my marriage.) I had just decided not to bother and was going to head back to my hotel, when a man came out. I asked him what the scene was like in there and if it was busy. He was a very welcoming spirit and obviously had just had his fill, so he was not looking for a pickup. I told him I had been in one of the other bath houses a few nights before and hated it and found that the Toronto gay scene had a real attitude. He agreed with me.

We ended up standing and talking for about 15 minutes. Somewhere in the conversation, he said he didn't drink, so didn't do the bar scene; and I said, "Neither do I." Then I said something about "one day at a time," and he asked me if I was into AA. I said, "I am," although I hadn't gone to many meetings in the past few years; and, of course, so was he. So, after a bit more conversation, I asked him if he wanted to go grab a coffee. Thus was the start of what turned out to be a very wonderful five days.

Ross was 47, Caucasian, about my height and build, looks much older than I do although we are only four months apart in age, and is a deeply spiritual, caring man. He was married for 22 years and has two teenage sons. He did a lot of volunteer work and worked part time in the insurance industry, earning a very modest income. He had MS and was slightly handicapped because of it. He walked with a slight limp and his face was not perfectly balanced. We found we were very compatible. He was the type of guy who will stop and give a panhandler something. He was very approachable and very much in love with life and humanity, as am I.

I was supposed to leave the next day but had flown down on points so I could easily change my ticket for no charge. I put off my departure "one day at a time" and didn't end up leaving Toronto until Saturday.

We met for supper Tuesday night. We went to a gay-friendly AA meeting Wednesday night. And on Thursday evening he took me to a "Gay Fathers" meeting. I walked into that room and felt the beautiful welcoming spirit of about 40 mature gay men with a balanced focus on life and their sexuality. It was a very spiritual and helpful meeting; and I felt so much a part of something healthy and good, not the spirit of the flighty gay bar scene crowd which I detest. After the meeting, we went out for coffee; I could hear a lot of stories. I met some great men, just solid, mature normal men who happened to be gay. I admit I, too, had bought into the stereotype of most queers as flighty bar flies looking for a quick blow job.

One fellow at the meeting mentioned that MCC [Metropolitan Community Church] was having a 25th anniversary celebration service on Friday night. I thought, "Good! I'll change my ticket for Saturday so I can go."

Well, that was the icing on the cake! I walked into that church and was immediately made to feel so welcome that I could hardly believe it. And if there weren't a couple of guys I had met at the "Gay Fathers" the night before! They asked me to sit by them. I literally sobbed my way through the entire service. It was so moving; I have never heard any congregation sing with such depth of feeling. They were singing the song of their acceptance found in that sacred place after undoubtedly years of rejection and pain. They simply glowed with joy and love.

I said to the guy sitting next to me, "I didn't bring my Kleenex box." They had one there for me in seconds. Turns out, Kleenex boxes are stationed at the end of every row! It was the most moving service I have ever experienced in my life. When they closed with, "When peace like a river attendeth my way, when sorrows like sea billows roll, whatever my lot, Thou has taught me to say, 'It is well, it is well with my soul,'" I must have used up half the box, as I sobbed along every word perfectly from memory. I could have never seen the words anyway through all the tears!

Afterwards, I said, "I don't know what got into me. I was just a bucket of tears." They waved their hands and said, "Oh, we all did that the first time we came to church here. Why do you think we have Kleenex boxes at the end of every row?" I knew I was home!

I met Ross again for coffee after MCC, as he was working on one of his volunteer jobs and couldn't attend with me. He ended up coming back to my hotel room where we spent the entire night talking, talking, and talking. I had to leave the next morning, and we knew we had to spend every minute of that countdown time together. By then we were so strongly drawn to each we could hardly stand it; but we kept chatting on and on. Finally I said, "What is happening here?" We fell into each other's arms in helpless surrender to our longings and held each other in a sweet embrace. We knew we were hopelessly in love.

We did not have sex. He respected my boundaries, which were crying to be torn away. Instead, we just sat and held and comforted each other in our arms. He and I have both felt nothing like this for anyone else ever in our lives. We both felt the presence of the God of love there in such an intense way that we were both in awe.

He ended up coming with me to the airport. We hugged and kissed as I prepared to go through that dark gate which rends loved ones from our sight in those cold airport surroundings, not caring in the least who saw or what anyone thought! I cried for over an hour on the plane and they must have thought I was going to a funeral! After I got home, Ross phoned, and he told me he went into the washroom and was crying so badly after I left that someone asked him if he was okay.

In our first phone conversation, which lasted about 90 minutes, we spent about two-thirds of the time discussing spiritual things. He told me he had never felt like that about anyone ever before. (Remember, he, too, had been married.) He told me that before he met me, he would have had to spell the word "monogamy" since he was so opposed to it he wouldn't say it. He told me he had never respected someone's boundaries and put aside his own selfish agenda and put someone else's welfare before his own. He told me he had felt the presence of God in the room with us as we hugged and held each other. He asked me if I was into some weird cult because he had met no one as deep as I was. He said he has been so full of love to everyone since that time that it is just spilling over everywhere to everyone he meets. He said he told his housemate, who is the manager of one of the popular bathhouses in Toronto, "I think you've lost a customer!"

And the strange thing was I felt exactly the same way. I no longer was drawn to surfing porn channels on the Internet. I looked at men differently, not with lust, but with appreciation and love. I had no desire to cruise or have a quick sex fix. My love cup was filled with that deep and total bond between Ross and me. And although we never had sex with each other, I was fully satisfied. I had finally loved and had been loved!

This experience showed to my heart as never before the power of genuine love to change me. I was a new man. Could the Creator have ever used a woman to reach me with love at this level? I have the most wonderful, tender, and caring wife imaginable. She sacrificed 24 years of her prime to save my life, but am I not capable of loving her on this complete level. I know the creator put Ross and me together to bring healing to my long battered spirit, and to help me accept myself finally totally and completely as a gay man.

That night I phoned Erin from my hotel room in Regina where I had stopped to see my grandmother on the way home. Erin said she was releasing me from the expectations of being a husband and would no longer have any sex with me. I felt a deep knife slowly extracting itself from my troubled, weary heart. It was a knife that had been there for 24 years, holding me down to the expectations of a wife toward a husband who could never possibly perform to the "standard." It felt so wonderful that I would never again have to play games in a role that was false. Never again would I have that deep underlying anxiousness about filling her needs as a hetero husband would do naturally in a way I never really could, though I tried so hard to be that kind of man for her for all those years.

I wept and wept and knew I was really free. I felt such a peace and joy afterward. I wanted to dance around the room and ended up before the mirror, standing naked, hard, eyes glowing in a way that I have never seen, much less imagined. I was free! I was at last in touch with the real me! I was no longer fragmented, anxious, or troubled, but perfectly free. I had finally realized that, as long as I was rejecting who I really am, I was actually rejecting the Creator who created me the way I am.

I came out fully and completely in that two weeks. For the first time in my life, I felt like a real mature adult man and not a clinging codependent little boy! It was wonderful. And, in that coming out process, the love and joy I felt left behind all the compulsions. I felt so full and accepting of myself that I did not need those things to fill that void to feel whole. I had been changed and had been made whole by a miracle of God's grace. It is a grace that had always accepted me just as I am, but that I refused to accept or believe. It took a gentle, handicapped man to lead me to accept that grace. God truly uses the weak things to confound the wise!!

That Monday evening, I came home to a new woman, fully centered in freedom of her new womanhood. I was stunned when she came to pick me up at the airport. She looked so different, so free, so confident, so charming, and beautiful. I had never seen her glow so wonderfully. And she was so full of the most incredible love that I could hardly believe it. The resents and hidden angers and frustrations were gone. We fell into each other's arms as precious friends who hadn't seen each other for years. But there was absolutely no sexual arousal for either of us in this tender exchange.

I came home a new man, proudly wearing a black T-shirt that said "Queerly Canadian" below a row of six little maple leaves in each of the rainbow colors, and a ball cap with the rainbow colors in little squares and rectangles of different sizes and shapes in an attractive arrangement. I left a child; I returned a man for the first time in my life!

She left that Thursday to go to a week-long intensive live-in counseling and therapy session. But, during the three days from the time I got home until she left, we had the most wonderful, deeply caring, loving, and harmonious relationship we had ever had between us in all those 24 years. We could finally be fully honest and accepting of each other. There were no games, no expectations—just perfect love and harmony. She will always be my best friend; but I knew I had to release her as well and let her find that beautiful, caring, hetero man who could truly love her fully. This pain was something we had both carried with us for 24 years. I feel sorry for any woman who is married to a gay man; for the journey and the end are only pain, for the woman as well as the man. Fortunately, we had no children to harm as well.

The night ended and the dancing day dawned, but we will never look back in regret. After all the things that happened in that two weeks, there was no doubt that there was a Creator behind all these "chance" happenings. The timing was perfect; we were both ready for the change at that point. Had I not gone to Toronto and Erin had come back from her treatment with the message, "It is over," I know my old childish self well enough to know that I would have killed myself.

Erin had lost faith in God years ago. For the first time in many years, she said something to me about God's leading. I smiled and said, "I think I just heard that 'God' word from you." She said, "Yes, I believe, once again, there is a

God." I was so thankful that her faith had finally been restored through all this. Mine had been deepened as never before.

We took the next year to ease through the transition of separating gently and slowly as a married couple, but we will be the closer forever. Realness and honesty are ties that ever bind more deeply than any piece of paper on a human-printed marriage certificate.

I know now I am alive because of the Creator's direct intervention in my life. All I want to do with the rest of my life is to be a channel of peace to the world as the beautiful, caring, loving, creative, gay man I am.

Yes, I believe in miracles, and I believe in change! Count me in on those change ministries! But I'm all for joining the one directed by the Creator. I am proud, grateful, and extremely happy to finally be really me! Thanks to all of you who have helped support me on my journey. This is a great fellowship for which I am deeply grateful.

Peter Williams is a pseudonym.

Female Hermaphrodite

By Pauline Wendy Phillips

On one grandma's side of the family, a legally blind scout for the Union during the Civil War once disguised himself in female clothing to escape the Confederates when he was in enemy territory. But I hardly think that counts in this story. Or does it?

I hope this expose of my 67 years of life from birth till 1999 will help transgenders/ intersexuals and their significant others, in general, transsexuals/ hermaphrodites/ pseudohermaphrodites and their significant others, in particular, and anyone else concerned with intersexism, transgenderism, or transsexualism in any way to deal with all transgenders/intersexuals in a caring, compassionate, constructive, loving, and positive manner.

Part I. The Early Years

As I recall, I was named "Paul," in part at least, after my other grandma's brother, Uncle Paul. He was a very sissy "man," and always cried over everything just like the rest of the women and girls did in the nineteenth century and later. He never married and was not a happy "man." I recall that someone in Grandma's family committed suicide, and I think it was him.

I was born at home in 1931 and was delivered by my father. He and my mother were finished or nearly finished with their study of chiropractic. At the time, it was illegal to practice chiropractic in Illinois. I received no more thorough examination to determine my sexual status than do most children born in a hospital. There were no x-rays. It was decided I was a boy, even though there were no visible testes. And these didn't descend on their own.

When I was born in Illinois, no birth certificate was required to be filed with the state. So my dad filled out a record of birth instead, which was filed with the county. The birth record showed I was male just because I had a small penis. Obviously, this birth record was inaccurate!

Time, mental and physical development, and research proved to me I was a 100% female-oriented hermaphrodite (HA) or female pseudohermaphrodite (FPHA). No actual medical tests were made to establish this exactly. Besides being saddled with hermaphroditism, I was born legally blind (20/200) as well. So whatever problems any transgenders (crossdressers, transsexuals, hermaphrodites, or pseudo-hermaphrodites) have, let them add on to it legal blindness and partial colorblindness, and they'll have a very good idea what my 66 years of life to date (1998) have been like!

My vision in both eyes is 20/200 or less, and I'm partially colorblind from a defective retina on both counts. I have too few cones, which provide details, distance vision, and accurate color detection. So I see mostly with rods–side and night vision. I can detect colors but can't tell for sure what some of them are. But, hey, I'm a survivor!

When I was around two, I got so severe a skin disease that no one but Mother thought I would survive. She fed me goat's milk, and I recovered; but ever after, my skin was extremely tender, more so than that of most women. Many years later, a nurse told me I bruised more easily than anyone she had ever seen! I lack some of the normal layers of skin. I wear slippers around home most of the time because of my extra tender skin.

About that same age, I fell down the basement stairs and landed on my head. Some doctors familiar with transgenderism say such brain-damaging accidents may contribute to changes in sexual/ gender identity. I certainly didn't need that besides!

When I was still young enough to use a potty chair, a hired teen girl who lived with us put me on the potty in the bathroom one day. Then I remember seeing her sitting on the toilet in front of me with her panties down. I'm sure a *real* boy baby wouldn't remember any such thing. What would be the point?

My favorite toy as a baby and small child was my rubber dolly. My brothers liked to take it and do weird things with it, which would make me cry. Then they and other members of the family would call me a sissy, pantywaist, and crybaby. For many years I was called such names, plus a weakling and tenderfoot, when I didn't say or do what was expected of me, or when I would try to express my female sexual identity.

When I was four, my elder sister, who was about ten, took me to a store that was giving one free toy to each poor child during the Great Depression. I had three brothers and three sisters, and we were poor then. I very much wanted a new and larger dolly, which I saw in the store; but my sister insisted I take a car or truck because she said dolls were only for girls. So, unhappily, I took a fire truck that I could ride; but I still wanted the doll.

One day when I was around age five, I was in the bathroom with my pants down and my eldest sister came in. She looked at me and said, "Let me see you." She inspected me, and then said, "You have no balls! I'm going to tell the folks." And she did.

I was laid on the dining room table, and Mother and Dad, by then both Doctors of Chiropractic, worked on me, massaging down what they assumed were testes. But by that time, my female sexual identity was already long since firmly established and could not be changed. My genital area looked like a closed vagina with abnormally small male sex organs protruding.

Years later, I read in a medical book that testes remaining undescended may dissolve away, remain sterile, or turn into ovaries; and that descended ovaries may dissolve away, remain sterile, or become testes. So which I really had at birth or developed later, before or after they were descended, is unknown. At least one was or became a testis, as I have two sons.

When I was around five, I was given a short-legged unlined wool suit to wear to church in the summer, and with no underwear. I spread my legs and held out my arms and cried and cried, but no one could figure out what all the fuss was about, even though I said, "It itches me!" So I was forced to be quiet and put up with my extreme misery. That I had had a skin disease that left me with abnormally thin skin failed to register with anyone, even with my mother!

When my youngest sister was old enough to play outside in warm weather, Mother gave her a pretty sunsuit to wear. I complained I wanted one, but it was denied me because I was supposed to be a boy. It was, however, cheaper for Mother to buy more than one item of a kind from the mail-order catalogs. And she used the hand-me-down system of dressing her children as much as possible. So she bought my sister and me (with my encouragement) look-alike shoes, uncuffed anklets, pants, striped shirts, pajamas, and underwear. Or she would give me such hand-me-down items from my sisters, or which had been bought at a rummage sale or the like.

One winter my youngest sister got a new bright blue two-piece snowsuit with a hood, which had a white furry trim. I very much wanted one for myself, but I had to be satisfied with an old, dark-colored, one-piece snowsuit. And during a program at the high school auditorium, I kept looking longingly at my sister's snowsuit and feeling I wasn't being treated right.

As long as she and I slept in the same room in the same bed, or later in separate beds, I recall no problem with our look-alike clothes. But at some point my eldest sister convinced my mother that I ought not to sleep in the same room with my sister. She was all worried about incest! And on that basis, from then on, I could never play in my sisters' bedroom or talk with them there. I managed it rarely. My mother's father's ancestors were Calvinists, as were the Puritans. That speaks volumes for itself!

So when I was made against my will to sleep in my brothers' bedroom with them, they teased me about wearing girls' pajamas because they opened up in the rear rather than the front. I don't recall any significant problem with teasing about wearing girls' panties—as I dressed and undressed with my back to them and my front toward the wall so they couldn't see my front; and I went to the bathroom alone as much as possible. I don't remember wearing boys' shorts regularly till I was in the tenth grade in high school and had to take a medical examination there.

One day after church I put on my elder sister's high-heeled dress shoes and came downstairs to the kitchen wearing them. She really got after me about it, made me take them off, and put them back in her closet! Now and then I also tinkered with some of Mother's things on her dressing table. She was tall and big, so I don't recall ever wearing any of her clothes.

In my years later library research on transsexualism/hermaphroditism, I read that one of the prime signs that a supposed boy is actually psychologically a girl, transsexual, or psychic-hermaphrodite was then thought to be the desire and practice of wearing female shoes or outer garments. The desire or practice of wearing female underwear first was then thought to show a crossdresser.

I remember wearing corduroy pants that zipped or buttoned up the side. I had no problem wearing girls' clothes myself as long as no one made fun of me. I also recall wearing panties in elementary school, taking care to hide the fact in the boys' restroom, whether I stood up or sat down. But before I left that school, all the doors on the stalls were removed from the boys' restroom except a reserved one for the janitor. From the boys' restroom I could look down a corridor and see the girls' restroom at the other end. I wanted to go in there to the girls' restroom when no one was around. I went once, at least part way.

For many years, when I would get cars or trucks for my birthday or for Christmas, I would run them into furniture, step on them, kick them around, throw them, or otherwise handle them roughly so that they would break apart or wear out quickly. When I played with them, or more preferably with my brothers' cars and trucks, I preferred to park them and then lie down beside them and imagine things or teach a much younger neighbor boy how to play with toys and make car noises. When my brothers asked me to play cars with them, I preferred to sit or lie down and watch them play while I would imagine things, and have shivers go down my spine. And my youngest brother particularly would get after me for just watching and not playing.

When I was about six, I was in a two-car accident on the way home from church. I was in the box of Granddad's pickup; and when my eldest brother, who at age 14 was driving it, ran into the left rear of my other granddad's car, I was thrown out and landed on my head. I received so severe a concussion that I wanted to sleep all the time for some time. And, as some medical specialists think that such injuries to the brain may contribute to changes in one's sexual identity, I didn't need that either!

When I was around eight, my two eldest sisters dressed me up in their clothes as a girl at bedtime and presented me to Granddad as "Pauline." When I was around 11 or 12, when Mother and Dad were away at a chiropractic convention, my youngest sister rather easily persuaded me to dress up in a dress and go down the street in broad daylight to a house in the next block to play with some other neighborhood kids in the yard of the home of my young boy playmate's grandmother whom I didn't really know. My sister assured me it would be all right, as we were only playing. My only concern was that I needed some panties to go with the dress, so she gave me a pair which had holes in them. The only reason I didn't do this sort of thing much more often was for fear of being ridiculed or punished.

I always preferred to play with my youngest sister, her girlfriend across the street, my female cousin, other neighborhood girls, their female friends, or their female relatives, rather than with my brothers or the neighborhood boys. The only exception was with the young boy playmate who could not fight with me. I had no interest in fighting or in boys' sports.

After playing with the girl across the street in her sandbox, et cetera, with or without my sister, for some years, her aunt finally told me through the kitchen window I should go play with boys. So I left very unhappy about it.

One evening during World War II I went with my sister to play with the young girl and boy up the street in their bedroom at their mother's invitation. Her husband was off as an officer in the navy. I noticed that the younger boy wore girls' silky panties. When we left and we outside, I asked my sister why he wore them. She said she didn't know. Evidently his mother used the hand-me-down system of clothing her children.

Once when I was playing with some neighborhood girls, a girl relative of one said I should leave and go play with the boys. The girl who lived at the house liked me, but she said nothing convincing to the girl that would keep me there. So I left very unhappy. Later, during World War II, when I was in the 8th grade, but not quite 13, a female classmate joined me in a war game at an intersection on one side of the street. The game opposed my youngest sister and another girl on the opposite side from the girl classmate and me. I concluded the girl with me liked me romantically, but I didn't worry about it. I was just glad to play with girls, regardless!

At a very early age, I took conscious note of the shoes, clothes, and jewelry of the neighborhood girls and at elementary school, much of which I still remember. In 6th grade, I asked the girl who sat next to me in one class about the ring she wore, which she said was a birthstone ring.

I especially remember the shiny T-strap black patent-leather flats with perforated toes worn with white cuffed anklets by two girl cousins of the girl who lived across the street from us. I really *loved* that shoe-anklet combination! And many years later, while still married, I bought a pair of T-strap flats for myself when the style was available in women's sizes for a few years. This close observation of what girls wore continued on into junior high, high school, junior college, and university.

The public elementary school I attended had a segregated playground for the boys and girls of grades six to eight at least. The girls in the front playground had swings, slides, merry-go-rounds, etc. The boys in the rear had football/

baseball grounds and basketball courts. I wanted to play with the girls on their ground, but I could not.

Some boys, including some younger than myself, liked to fight me or corner me. When I wouldn't fight back, they called me a sissy and a weakling. Two of my brothers tried to teach me how to wrestle, fight, and box in their bedroom; but I just wasn't interested in any of this either for play or defense. At the time, I didn't really understand my true psychological make-up or refused to admit any more for fear of ridicule; and so I attributed my lack of interest in boys' sports and fighting to my religious convictions. But it was a much deeper mental process than that.

My doctor parents had some medical books stored in the attic. Its entrance was in the ceiling of the closet to my and my brothers' bedroom. We sometimes got these books and looked at the pictures of all the weird babies and people—the kind that used to be found in circuses. There were hermaphrodites, Siamese twins, two-headed, three-legged, animal-hairy, scaly hide, etc.

When I was around 12—the age when some girls then began to be interested in boys—the boy I liked the best hit me and knocked me down. It made me feel terrible! I wasn't hurt physically, really, but emotionally. I just sat up right where I was knocked down near the baseball catcher's fence and cried inside, if not outwardly. Finally, the boy came over to me and made up with me, saying he was sorry, and I felt much better.

My grandma liked me to walk around town with her. She once noticed I walked by stepping out on my heels. She said I should walk by stepping out on my toes or ball of the foot like she did. She showed me how to do it and then tried to get me to walk like that. It was hard for me to do then, and I gave up on it. I didn't want any criticism or ridicule from walking like women or girls, anyway. But I naturally walk like females now without thinking about it.

In late elementary school, my youngest brother and I had to chop and saw wood for our central-heating furnace. My hands were still growing, so this kind of work enlarged them beyond what a girl my age normally had.

Virtually all the pictures taken of me from babyhood, as a child, and as a teen show me as pouting, solemn, disgusted, or perhaps even angry. I didn't *want* my picture taken! As I recall, the only picture of me as a child that I liked and in which I was really smiling was taken by my dad of me and my youngest sister, with me seated on a tricycle and her standing on the rear axle step. We both played together outside like that.

Whatever pictures I ever had of me dressed as a male have long since been destroyed. And, when my mother died, I told my eldest sister that as far as I was concerned all pictures Mother had of me dressed as a male could be destroyed, as I didn't want any of them.

In junior high in Southern California, my mother gave me a new boy-girl-look-alike girl's coat for my birthday or Christmas. A boy noticed it buttoned up the "wrong way," and asked me if I were a hermaphrodite. To escape criticism, I said Mother gave me the coat, and that I wasn't a hermaphrodite. Girls then would ask me to walk home from school with them or play with them, and I refused. I was confused! But still longed to be with them.

In the 8th grade in junior high, I hated to have to undress in the boys' gym and shower in a mass public shower. We had to wear gym shorts to play. So I started wearing mine under my pants. This helped some, but didn't cure the shower problem at the end of P.E. Because of my poor vision, I finally got an excuse from my mom, a chiropractor, to not have regular P.E.

I still had to dress down to my shorts, but didn't need to shower, or did so early, after talking to the teacher. I don't recall what I said, but he was nice about it. It all worked out so that I could wear some old panties under my gym shorts. My mother gave me the old panties that my sister had when I complained my rear was cold in the winter. I hadn't been wearing boys' undershorts.

In junior high, I particularly noticed the clothes, shoes, and activities of the band/ cheerleader baton twirlers. This group practiced outside where I would walk along to my next class early or from carrying a note from my teacher to someone. The girls all wore shiny black patent leather sandals with white cuffed anklets. I thought that sandal-anklet combination looked *so* nice, as well as the rest of their outfits! And I wanted to wear them and be a band/ cheerleader baton twirler. I wasn't allowed to attend junior high school dances, but I would look in the open door to the girls' gym where they were held and watch awhile.

Once, the junior-high girl who lived across the fence to our backyard invited me to go into her house and play with her. I wasn't sure whether she meant regular play or romance. I wanted to go anyway but refused because my mother had told me not to play with the neighbor kids without her knowledge or permission.

Before starting high school, I went to Sears to buy some new clothes. The salespersons in the big boys' clothing department insisted I get the extra-long legged blue jeans they both said were popular right then. I tried them on, and the legs turned up made a cuff around six inches long. And the inside blue was much lighter than the outside blue.

I liked neither the cuff length nor the color contrast. I thought they looked hickish. I hated them and refused to buy them. City girls I knew didn't dress that way. I insisted on jeans with legs short enough that no turn-up was needed. I recall the saleslady saying the only jeans that short were girls' jeans. I recall replying that if they looked alike, what difference did it make. She went off and brought back some shorter-leg jeans. I tried them on, and they were fine. She evidently got them from the girls' department! The label said Sears.

In high school, two girls who were friends, who sat behind me in Biology class, wore identical white heel-strap sandals, which I liked. Other girls wore white wedge-heel slip-on flats I liked. Some Hispanic girls wore huarache sandals, which I noted. Much later, the girl I liked best wore medium-dark, high wedge-heel shoes that looked like the toes might be perforated. Being legally blind, I couldn't tell for sure. But I liked them.

One day when she was working on a class project after school, I walked down the hall and saw her shoes in the hall by a classroom door. I quietly walked up, kneeled down, and inspected her shoes. The toes had small metal pieces attached. Obviously, no non-transgender, non-crossdresser, non-transsexual, non-hermaphrodite genuine teen-age male would carry on like that!

When I was old enough to apply for a Social Security card in order to get a work permit, shortly before my 14th birthday, as I recall, I still had no birth certificate, which was required to get the card. So my mother showed me the record of birth she had and sent the required information back to Illinois so a birth certificate could be made. She had previously learned that Illinois had collected all the records of birth from the individual counties in the state, and for a small fee would prepare birth certificates upon request.

I recall telling her how I should be a girl and have a girl's name, but it did no good. I recall asking the lady at the Social Security office when I applied for my card whether I could be on record as a girl with a girl's name—Pauline. But she said not without testing or information I was sure my folks wouldn't or couldn't supply.

So I finally gave in to the idea of being male and for some years repressed my female feelings. But they all reappeared later in full force!

When I was a child of pre- and elementary-school age, I was also known as terrible tempered. I insisted for so long, to no avail, that I was a girl or should have been that I finally gave up talking about it, mostly. So I used anger as an emotional outlet for the great stress I was under for not being able to dress and live as a girl. I was an unhappy child and pouted whenever pictures were taken of me.

Eventually, my religious convictions toned down my anger to hardly anything. Instead, I used strategy to get around things I'd otherwise get mad about. Then felt glad I could outsmart those in my family who tried to run my life.

Once, when I was talking to my "old maid" algebra/geometry teacher, I had to go to the restroom. The boys' restroom was down the hall a way, but not very far. She gave me the key to the closer restroom for female teachers, since the girls' restroom was on the other side of the building. I already knew where her restroom was, as I had cleaned it along with the girls' and boys' restrooms in virtually the entire school as a janitor's assistant in 9th grade.

Once, when I was working inside a stall in the girls' restroom, two girls came in and used two other stalls. I overheard them talk about their sex life! Normally there was a sign up on a chain across the door when I was in the restroom. But either I forgot to hook it up, or they had to go badly enough that they came in anyway when they didn't see anyone around.

This job as janitor's assistant made my clothes dirty, especially from emptying pencil sharpeners. And I didn't have enough changes of clothes to stay clean at school before work after school. I didn't like this. Once, two girls coming out of the restroom commented to each other about how dirty I was. Fortunately, I worked as a janitor for only one year. After that I wore cleaner and nicer clothes, unfortunately male.

When my elder sister and her husband came to visit us when I was in high school, I did a lot of the cooking. I also liked to lean on things rather than stand up straight. Was it subconsciously to make me look shorter like a girl? They gave me a homemade card, I guess, for my birthday. It read in part "Paul-lean Cookshack Phillips." The pronunciation of "Paul-lean" sounds the same as "Pauline" that I had been called by my elder sister's years earlier at age eight. I noted that!

My youngest sister liked me to walk around town with her. Her excuse was that she was scared to be alone, or that she wanted me to appear to be her boyfriend before she had one of her own. It wasn't too hard for her to convince me to go with her. One day we walked around the corner up a side street of the next block from our home.

Down a driveway we saw four young neighbor sisters my sister played with playing in their backyard on or near the fence dividing their yard from the one on the street we were on. So we walked down the driveway, and my sister talked with them awhile. Finally, the eldest girl around my sister's age said I shouldn't be with them, that I was supposed to be with boys. So I walked away much disappointed.

When I was in junior college, white saddle shoes with black, brown, or red were popular with the girls. Some guys wore them in men's sizes as well, especially if their girlfriends did. The ones I liked were the girls' that had white-edge thin soles that came only to the very side of the shoe. I never liked shoes or sandals of any style that had wide soles that went beyond the edge of the shoe/sandal. That made them look unnecessarily wide to me.

There was a shoe store on a corner where I waited for the bus to go practice the pipe organ. I often would look in the windows at the girls' and women's shoes while I waited and wished I could wear the girls' saddle shoes I liked.

I once commented to my organ teacher that girls must be able to play the pedal board easier than males because their feet were smaller and narrower, and their shoes had thinner and narrower soles. He agreed they had an advantage, unless a male wore organ shoes made for playing the organ. The organ shoes, for both men and women, have thin and narrow soles for feeling for notes and for ease in playing, and 1 1/8″ heels to play thirds with the heel and toe of the same foot.

I remember one girl who sat beside me in history class. She had nice, long, shiny blond hair and nice clothes. But she always wore beat-up dirty saddle shoes. I could never figure out why she did that! Why didn't she wear nice clean saddle shoes like all the other girls, was my question? I wanted to ask her, but never did. I envied the girls who wore nice dresses, skirts, blouses, sweaters, and shoes to college; and I noticed what they wore.

When I was at the university, perforated-toe T-strap flats in patent leather or other colors, including white, were popular with some girls. I liked these very much—and the girls in my classes who wore them. Earlier I had bought a pair for myself, while I was still married.

My interest in girls from elementary school through university was virtually limited to girls who were very short, or at least small-boned–that is, childlike or girl-like in appearance–including the girl I married. When I held her on my lap while dating or after marriage, I felt I was like a mother to her. When I was around 14, I wanted to hug, kiss, mother, and play with (babysit) in the backyard a cousin's two baby girls. But when she saw me, she drove me away, saying I should leave them alone. I kissed both girls before she saw me with them.

Shortly after World War II was over, Mother bought her sons white 100% nylon dress shirts, and nylon sport shirts soon were available. My elder brother and I continued to wear these after polyester-cotton shirts were worn by men. I liked the nylon shirts best because they felt better on my abnormally tender skin. My brother wore them because he had asthma and said he was allergic to cotton. We liked them also because they were wash-and-wear.

When I studied piano by home study around age 14 on, I had trouble reaching octaves. So I stretched and exercised my hands while they were still growing so I could reach the octaves. The result, along with the work I did, is that my hands are larger than they otherwise would have been, and my thumbs don't spread out normally.

About the same time, Dad had me help my brother dig up and chop out two large tree stumps in the backyard before the house was added on to, and later one in the front yard. This use of the ax likewise enlarged my hands. Also, the pressure and weight on my feet from all this digging and chopping while I was still growing enlarged them somewhat beyond the average woman's size for my build.

Holding several jobs later in which I had to stand all day on my feet added to this foot enlargement, especially the job where I had to lift heavy packages of paper for a paper cutter. This standing all day and having gone barefoot every summer from babyhood and as a child, later flattened my feet and lengthened them beyond what girls' feet normally were.

In junior high, high school, junior college, and university, I still wasn't interested in boys' sports. By then I was attributing it partly to being legally blind. So I got a doctor's excuse from Mother to go to the library or handicapped P.E. class instead. I never had a date with a girl while in high school or junior college, nor even kissed one, and remained a virgin till I married at age 24. And at the university after my wife divorced me, I didn't date girls either, although I made a weak stab at it.

I wanted a short girl in high school as my best girlfriend but was so shy I never could say or do anything to show her I even liked her. I'd even repeat over and over to myself as I rode my bike home from school what I wanted to say to her, and fantasized about walking her home from school, but none of this ever did any good. When we were seniors, she sat next to me in one class and asked me in a whisper the answer to a question in the test we were taking. Immediately, I dropped all interest in her and attributed it to my high sense of honesty. But I'm sure a genuine male would have acted differently in the whole affair from beginning to end.

When I graduated from high school at age 17, the yearbook picture of me revealed I had a small feminine neck. When I graduated from junior college, I destroyed the yearbook except for the picture of my organ teacher seated at the pipe organ, and a copy of the senior insignia for our class sweaters I had designed with his help. He also taught art. When I was given a photocopy of my graduating class 25 years later after I'd begun living as a woman, I cut the picture of myself out and destroyed it but kept the others.

When I would tell Mother that I thought I really was or wished I were a girl, or while in junior college that I *should* have been a girl, she would ask, "Why?" So I would explain what was on my mind. Her typical response was, "Well, you're not, so that's that!"

In Junior College, a male fellow music student who befriended me invited me to his apartment at noontime. After we got there together, he asked me if I was gay. I said no, but I later assumed he was, as he had nothing to do with me afterwards outside class, even though I had let him know I wanted us to be friends.

Part II. Love and Loss

When I became an adolescent and began to develop sexually, I developed all the secondary female sex characteristics except a bust. I developed female spine curvature, hips, waist, rear, and pubic dimples on the lower back, indicating female muscular development. And my pants had to be drawn in at the waist 2″ to 3″ inches by a tailor to make them fit. And my belt became too big. So I punched more holes in it, then later got a smaller belt. I wore big-boy-size shirts and pants long after my age suggested I should wear men's sizes. Male clothing salespeople commented on this. My weight got up to 175 lbs. when I was a junior in high school, but I lost 10 lbs. from a week-long illness, and never gained it back till long after marriage. As an adult, when I bought a new suit for my brother's wedding, the salesperson commented on how hard it was to fit me.

I grew no hair on my chest like Dad or my brothers, except a few hairs around my nipples, which many girls and women normally have. With my female muscular development, all efforts at a health ranch to "build me up" or my own efforts to take a muscle-building course failed, except to strengthen my arms.

My arms or legs were not male-like hairy. I was slow in growing facial hair and postponed shaving as long as I could until a male high school classmate asked me when I was going to shave. I don't recall having any noticeable pubic hair until after I was married; and then, except for a few stray hairs, it was essentially triangular (female), rather than diamond-shaped (male).

After marriage, when hair appeared noticeably on my legs for the first time, I shaved it off just as I had seen my wife do; she got after me and said not to do it anymore. So I didn't, but I still wanted to. Both my parents and each of my three brothers and three sisters were tall, the males being 6′ or taller. But my enlarged feet were still very much smaller in length and width than Dad's or my three brothers, all of whom had large feet.

When I became employed at the health ranch and began to buy my own clothes, and no longer lived with my parents, I began to wear look-alike sandals and shoes for men and women. I wanted to wear the actual women's style and size but held back. When I put up such a fuss at Sears about the men's slip-on shoes I was trying on being too wide, I'm sure the salesperson sold me a women's look-alike pair and size which fit right. They were an 8D. But from their physical size, cut, appearance, and fit I was certain they were the women's style and size. After fitting them on me, he told me to wait, and after some time he returned with the shoes. I figured he did something to the labeling inside to disguise the fact that they were women's shoes. When I got back to the ranch, the owner's sister commented my shoes looked too small, but I assured her they fit fine. I *wanted* the salesperson to sell me women's shoes without me asking for them!

When I moved into my youngest sister's former bedroom when she was away at college, I noticed a pair of her old size 8B saddle shoes in a box in the closet, and I tried them on. They fit somewhat tight. Later, I buckled my belt up very tight around my waist in bed, wishing I had even a smaller waist.

About then, I forced my small penis (when hard) up into my skin-covered vagina-like cavity. It was hard going at first, but suddenly something gave way inside, and it was easy after that to hide it there, whether it was hard or soft. I figured that what split was the same thing more or less as the barrier in most virgin females' vaginas.

When I returned home from working at the health ranch, I looked in the catalogs for some women's penny loafers to wear to work. I tried to hide just what I was looking for when anyone came around, but my brother (whom I later learned was a crossdresser) seemed to take more interest in what I was doing than I thought was "normal" for a man. Perhaps he had taken a liking to the small shoes I was already wearing to work. They were the ones that I got at Sears when I worked at the ranch. When the shoes came in the mail and I tried them on, my brother seemed to be there, taking it all in and asking questions.

After I got a city job, I began buying women's loafers, size 9A, and wearing them to work. Both men and women commented favorably about them. My justification for this was that my feet were too narrow to wear men's or even boys' shoes. The size 9A shoes were too tight to walk to and from the Pacific Electric depot or to stand in all day. I got ingrown toenails and blisters. I even put pieces of metal in the back inside my socks to keep the top of the backs from cutting into my heel. So I later got size 9B.

At the health ranch's dairy, I had met a large Dutch woman working there who said her feet were so large that she had to wear men's shoes, the largest women's size then being size 9. So I figured I could do the same thing in reverse. I adopted literally the saying, "If the shoe fits, *wear* it!"

One day when I walked home after work from the P.E. station behind two girls, I noticed how they stepped up onto the curb with their toes rather than with their heel or whole foot, tensing their foot in the process to help raise them up. I wanted to step up the same way and began to imitate that way of stepping.

For a while I was on an organic-food kick, and I gradually lost weight till I weighed only around 145 lbs. or less. I wore men's socks for many years, but I liked them to be nylon, orlon, or acrylic rather than cotton or wool.

Once I tried selling vitamins house to house. In the company sales headquarters building, I once saw a sales representative there who had tiny feet. So I felt justified all the more to wear women's shoes.

One day I was sitting on my bed in my bedroom and my girlfriend was sitting on a chair. When I asked her then to marry me, at first she said no. She said that although she felt honored I had asked her, she didn't love me enough. So I told her I loved her enough to marry her even if she didn't love me. This broke down her defense, and she agreed to marry me. But ever after I had the fear in the back of my mind that eventually she would either quit loving me or find a man she loved more and leave me.

Before I married, I called my fiancée's attention to the fact that I wore women's penny loafers. I compared them with the men's shoes in a mail-order catalog. I said I didn't want to have any secrets between us. My excuse for wearing such shoes was because I had small feet, that men's shoes were too wide or otherwise ill-fitting. And she accepted the idea, saying that the men's and women's loafers looked about the same. However, the loafers I wore had thinner soles than men's loafers or other men's shoes had then. And the top was lower cut than the men's shoes.

After I became engaged, my fiancée returned to her home state of Texas. She knew I had worn women's loafers in the past. I once wrote her I hadn't gotten my laundry done. And that if she had been here (California), I could have borrowed a pair of her panties to wear. When she got my letter, she read it while she was standing in the cafeteria line at work. She laughed so hard about what I said that someone asked her what she was laughing about. She replied something vague to cover up what she had read.

Our courtship and marriage were accomplished under abnormal cultural, social, religious, and environmental circumstances. She had to suggest or first move on almost everything except taking a car ride or a walk. I acted more like best girlfriend to best girlfriend than boy to girl or man to woman. And both of us were abnormally naïve about sexuality to deal properly with the situation, although both of us sensed at some point that something was not "right." I had blocked many of my childhood experiences from my mind and didn't relate them to my situation then.

But because of our religious beliefs we went ahead despite the sexuality/gender problems. While dating my girlfriend, and later fiancée, I had had plenty of opportunities to have sex, but never did. When I confessed once that earlier I had felt like having sex one night out in the grass, she said she had wanted me to. I told myself my refraining from having sex was due to not believing premarital sex was right. But there was much more to it than that.

Shortly before we married, my fiancée measured me for a new suit for our wedding. As she did so, she commented about my small waist, wide hips, and protruding rear, and that she thought I needed to gain weight.

On our wedding day, I offered my fiancée the chance to back out of marrying me if she wanted to, but she wanted to go ahead with our marriage plans. I thought marriage might solve my sexuality/gender problems. But, even though we had very many happy times together for several years, marriage was really the beginning of sorrows—for both of us! I wanted to be and dress more and more female more of the time in more places than she would allow. I also liked to sit down to urinate. My excuse was that it was cleaner because nothing splashed onto the walls, the floor, or my clothes.

We talked over the matter of crossdressing considerably. And during my eight years of marriage I endlessly questioned my wife about virtually everything female and feminine. I watched her like a hawk to learn as much as was possible to learn. Since my grandmothers, mother, sisters, and teachers didn't teach me how to act and dress as a girl or a woman, except for one grandmother trying to teach me how to walk, I used my wife to teach me. I learned a great deal. And quickly. And remembered it. And now for over 29 years I have lived by it.

After I married, I immediately was not satisfied to just wear women's loafers, which were a 10 AA then. I wanted to and began to wear women's panties, elastic briefs, pajamas, pulled-up-cuffs cuffed anklets, boots, and slippers. When my wife bought a new long elastic brief, I asked her what she was going to do with the old one. She said it was for me. So I wore it regularly till it was completely worn out.

Once when I was dressed in a regular elastic brief over my panties with my penis tucked inside me, when we were lying on the bed, she tried to get into my panties to make love. But it was hard going for her! Once I bought my wife a package of new satin nylon panties of various colors, which she was glad to get. But when I told her I had also gotten a similar package of nylon panties for myself, she said that took away some of the happiness she had from getting hers. I once told her later that I liked my panties to be a size smaller than recommended. She said she did, too.

Then I began to wear women's thongs, sandals, and canvas shoes which were near enough in style and color to men's that I thought I could get by without negative comment. If anyone did comment, either men or women, it was always complementary or just that I had small shoes, such as my male cousin did when I visited him. My response to such comments was that I had small feet.

I also wore clear or pink-tinted nail polish on long fingernails. In high school and junior college, I had studied the pipe organ, then quit it for a time. But after I began to play the organ again, I kept my fingernails short. One can't have everything!

Once I got some women's sandals that had a snap-on heel strap. I removed the strap and used the sandals as house slippers. Later I got another even more feminine-looking pair of sandals and cut the heel strap off and used them for house slippers. My crossdresser brother came in one day while I was putting them on and asked me if they came big enough to fit him! I said, "I don't think so." The sandals were a women's size 8 M, and he wore a men's size 10 or larger shoe.

Once when my wife and I visited friends, a married couple, the wife wore T-strap flats. The light in the room was fairly bright, and I had my sunglasses with me. So I used the light as an excuse to wear them in the living room. Then, with some excuse, I sat down on the floor from my chair. My real purpose was to get a good look at the woman's T-strap flats without being detected!

Partly because of my legal blindness, I hadn't been able to get a job for some time; so my wife had me wash her nylon hose as well as do the rest of the laundry and look after our two sons. When my wife was at work, I began wearing under my pants my regular sheer gala-color (the lightest, most nude available) seamless nylon hose I bought at Penney's. And I wore women's T-strap flats in the house and out to the garbage can. I tried on as much of my wife's clothes as I could get on even though they were too small. Washing her nylons and her underclothes helped me to want to do this, and to wear more women's clothes of my own.

I didn't understand my compulsion to wear women's clothes, and I thought I must be the only person in the world like that! When my wife would mention magazine articles she had read or heard about describing crossdressers or gay men, I would stoutly, sincerely, and truthfully deny that I was either of these. Yet, despite all my history, I was not willing to admit then to myself that I was really a woman inside. I had been criticized and ridiculed so much that I had consciously and/or unconsciously hidden the facts, similar to what a sexually abused child does. At the time, I didn't recall many of the details given here, nor relate them together.

I just didn't know what to think about myself; and because of the criticism and ridicule I had already received so much, I built myself a shell and crawled inside. And for years, I put up a masculine front to most people, but my marriage revealed the truth and tore my shell away. I justified wearing nylon panties because of my very tender skin and because I had piles that caused rectal itch.

My wife thought nylon shirts looked sissy and didn't like me to wear them. Some of them were the see-through type to a greater or lesser extent. Once when she and I were going out somewhere in Los Angeles, I met her in L.A. In the car she said I smelled nice, so I hastened to say that I had had no cologne, so I used some of hers. She didn't respond, so I repeated what I said.

She had already committed herself, so what could she say? So instead she noticed I was wearing a nylon dress shirt, so she got after me for wearing it. That fact that my brother wore nylon shirts all the time to church and to work didn't cut any ice with her. Nylon shirts were sissy to her, and that was that! Most women and/or men must have thought the same way, because most men quickly gave them up after the cotton-polyester blend wash-and-wear shirts became available.

I also began to wear heavyweight nylon beige women's long hose, which required wearing a garter belt or girdle, and long panties to cover up the lump of the garters under my pants. One day in the car my wife noticed my hose and remarked unkindly, "The next thing you'll want to wear a dress!" I sat silently without replying, for I knew it was true.

About that time, I got an adjustment in my youngest brother's chiropractic office. He commented on my smooth, shiny socks as I lay on the adjusting table. I just said I was wearing long hose. So he pushed up my pant legs quickly to have a look, then pushed them back down. But thankfully, he said nothing more.

One time when I went into my folks' bedroom, a dresser drawer was open. I saw some of Dad's shorts. They were made of rayon and had a Ward's label. I wondered if that was because he had piles. But his undershirts were rayon as well. So I wondered later if he might have inherited some mild femininity from his mother—and passed mine on to me. At some point I began wearing rayon, and later nylon, shorts and undershirts part of the time before I began wearing women's underwear. One guy I knew who saw me wear rayon shorts said I had real feminine shorts! I replied they were only rayon like my dad wore.

I was still a virgin when I married and never had much interest in sex after marriage. I lost most of my personal interest in it after the novelty wore off. I thought it was all too much work and wanted to be on the bottom rather than the top! I seldom got to be on the bottom.

One of the hardest ideas for me to relate to was that I, as professedly male, should show a close interest in only one girl at a time and exclude all others.

So when my brothers or male classmates would ask me about my love life, I would say there was plenty of time, or stupid remarks like, "I wouldn't want to date or kiss a girl I didn't want to marry," as if one could tell that in advance. And after marriage, I still wanted to be close friends with several girls or young women, married or not.

After I married, at some point I went to a men's shoe store and tried on some shoes. They were all still too wide. So I felt justified in continuing to wear women's loafers. A few years later, I bought some boys' size loafers from the Sears catalog. They were too wide as well. So I felt all the more justified in wearing females' shoes. Of course, I knew there were shoe stores in L.A. or elsewhere who sold hard-to-find sizes. But I was unwilling to pay more for such shoes–since I really *wanted* to wear women's shoes, anyway!

For about the last four years of my marriage, I ate or drank certified raw whole milk, half-and-half, cream, cottage cheese, and ice cream, which I could metabolize better than pasteurized milk or cream. Cream, half-and-half, and whole milk contain cow estrogen. This helped to feminize my body and mind even more. I even started growing breasts at about age 30! But when I called my wife's attention to that, she said they were only fat! I was 5′ 11.5″ then, and my weight got up to about 190 lbs. This overweight obscured my female hip-waist-rear lines somewhat, as being overweight often does with women.

After about six years of marriage, one night my wife began crying in bed. When I asked her what was wrong, she said she had fallen in love with a man we both knew and liked from her work, but that she didn't want to hurt me. I told her I still loved her, anyway. In my mind, I had long since expected this to happen someday. So I wasn't surprised or caught off guard.

She stayed at work late more often and later. Finally, she told me not to call her at work at night because she didn't want anyone to know she was working alone. I suspected she was doing more than work, but I didn't accuse her. Once she came home late and lay down on the couch instead of going to bed with me, despite all my urging her to do so. I got up in the middle of the night, and she was still there asleep on the couch. So I put a blanket over her. I was sure she had been unfaithful to me, but I said nothing.

Later, she would talk on the phone and giggle with the very tall, handsome man we both liked. He was her boss by then. He would also come by and pick her up to take her to work so they wouldn't both have to take cars. I didn't like any of this, but I refrained from saying much. I liked the man a lot myself! So what could I say?

One night when my wife came home from work late, I was watching TV. She said to turn it off as she wanted to talk to me. She then told me she was leaving me. We talked the matter over some. Then she got up from her chair and went into the bedroom. I went outside and stood by a window and cried and cried till I couldn't cry anymore! I tried to cry quietly so neither my wife, sons, family in the adjoining house, nor the neighbors could hear. No one said anything about my crying, so I guess I succeeded. As best I can recall, I've never really cried as much since.

When my wife left me, and then got a divorce after eight years of marriage, none of the reasons she gave for doing so was specifically attributed to my wearing women's clothes; but I suspected that was undoubtedly part of it. Her principal reason was that she was unhappy. So when I got rid of all my women's clothes by giving them to the Salvation Army, and told her so, she replied she didn't like that either, because I'd just replace them. And I did—after the divorce was final or close to it. The medical books on transsexualism, which I later studied, say that replacement is always done when a transsexual gets rid of women's clothes.

When my wife left me, I was unemployed. She took custody of my two sons. I didn't contest it due to both my income level—legal blindness disability income from the state—and my crossdressing, which I didn't want to come to light in court. I feared it would if my wife or her lawyer thought it necessary.

Likewise, while I consulted two lawyers on contesting the divorce, in the end I didn't contest it in court when my wife told me plainly to my face the night before the court session, "I don't love you, and that's *that*!" Again, I didn't want my intersexualism to come to light in court. It wasn't so well known then via the media. I feared several repercussions.

Fortunately, my wife didn't ask me to pay any child support or alimony, since I was unemployed and getting blind disability money from the state. But later, after I became a student at California State University at Long Beach, I could get federal disability Social Security, which not only added to my disability income, but paid money to both sons till each was 22 and had graduated from the same university I had attended!

After we separated, I returned to college, which the state was willing to pay for because of my legal blindness, providing I would train to be a blind teacher. And while attending CSULB, I started wearing women's clothes again; I told myself, "I'll be my own woman!" This statement didn't reveal my true feelings, but it was as close as I was willing or able to put into words or thoughts at the time. My romantic interest in girls there was of no success either.

Being short of money, I ate less food, and gradually lost a lot of the weight I had gained, but *not* my bust. It was more than just fat. At some point I began to wear waist whittlers to reduce the size of my waist. I wore them both day and night, but particularly at night in bed, when I was less active and wouldn't notice any discomfort in my sleep. I got a size smaller than recommended whenever I could.

After my wife's divorce was final and she remarried, after I began to wear women's underclothes, shoes, and man-tailored women's clothes at the university, I did a *lot* of library research at CSULB in Long Beach, CA, where I was a student. I had taken a master's level course in library research. I did this research on transsexualism and hermaphroditism. I researched the medical books in the university library about my problem. Later, when I moved to L.A., I continued this research in the L.A. public, USC, UCLA, and UCLA medical libraries. I also bought some books on transsexualism.

I checked out so many sex-oriented medical books that the check-out girl began to question me why I was checking out so many of those books! I said I was doing research. In my research I learned that all my experience, my feelings, and my physical characteristics added up to the fact that I was more than what some would call a transsexual or psychic-hermaphrodite, and that a large percent of so-called transsexuals exhibit secondary female sex characteristics just as I did.

I learned that the only successful treatment for male-to-female (M2F, MTF) transsexualism was female-hormone therapy, electrolysis hair removal, and sex reassignment plastic surgery; and that there were many more transsexuals similar to me and intersexuals like me, which made me feel better. But my research on hermaphroditism at the same time revealed fully to my mind that I was, in fact, a 100% female-oriented hermaphrodite, or at least a female pseudohermaphrodite, both being genetically female.

So I had facial hair removed by an understanding lady electrologist in Los Angeles who worked on entertainment people and others like me. After a few treatments, before she worked on my face, she looked it over carefully, closely, close enough for us to kiss. She would then ask me if I had any special requests. She had told me about her life, and we had become friends. From what she had said, I thought she might like me in a romantic sense, even though she knew of my intersex status. I wasn't certain whether she was asking me about my face or about romance. So I would answer, no, just the regular thing.

Thus I had "grow-your-beard day for electrolysis tomorrow." One day I came home on the bus still with some facial hairs that the lady hadn't removed. At the bus stop near Sears a man whom I was sure was gay took great interest in me. To get away from him, I went into Sears to buy some hangers, taking the escalator to the second floor. He followed me in all the way up and talked to me on the way and after I got there!

Another "beard day" I stood in front of a barber shop waiting for the bus. I had hairs on my face. A man stopped his car and walked over to me and tried to get me to go with him. I think he offered me money. When I refused, he asked why I looked or dressed that way. I suspected he was gay or a plain-clothes police.

After several treatments, I told the lady I wanted to come dressed as a woman. That was okay with her, and she told me about the restroom facilities. So I put face powder on my face extra heavy and thick to cover my day-old beard. Many of my hairs were white or light, so it wasn't much trouble to cover them. A few hairs were bright red—my Welsh Celtic ancestry, you know! She would complain that my hairs were almost too short for her to remove.

On "beard day" before I could dress regularly as a woman, I wore man-tailored women's clothes—pants—and carried a ladies' colorful billfold in my hand rather than a purse. Because I had to pay cash, which I had little of, I quit the treatments before the job was fully completed, but enough to get by.

In the late 1960s I began to contact—by mail, phone, or in person—doctors, surgeons, and psychiatrists and psychologists who were familiar with my problem, including Dr. Benjamin. I got an estrogen (Premarin) prescription and examination from Dr. Barbosa in Tijuana, Mexico, whom I had visited dressed as a woman.

Later, I got a prescription from Dr. Elmer Belt in Los Angeles, which he sent to me by mail without me going to his office. I wasn't able to afford surgery, but since my small penis fit up into my vaginal cavity when dressed, I could get by. After reading his book on transsexualism, I wrote to Dr. John Money at Johns Hopkins University, Baltimore, MD, that I believed I was, in fact, a hermaphrodite. But he doubted it because of its falsely supposed rarity.

I first took the Mexican Premarin at the Greyhound bus station on the California side of the border. When I went to the bathroom later at home in Long Beach, there was a great deal of foam in the toilet from my urine that looked just like foamy albumen from egg yolks. (I once used such in a print shop on zinc offset printing plates to sensitize them to hold words and images exposed via bright lights from negatives.) I had previously eaten eggs regularly.

So the estrogen really cleaned out my bloodstream! Later I got blood clots in my eyes, so I cut down on the daily dose. After I began taking Premarin, I noticed I was attracted to student guys with hairy arms at the university. But when I quit taking it later, my interest in girls returned.

I had a psychiatric evaluation done at UCLA Medical Center by Dr. Richard Green who co-authored Dr. Money's book, and also took tests with a psychologist there. The state of Illinois where I was born provides for sex and name change because of surgery on birth certificates. So it's easy to see how frustrating and depressing it was for me not to afford surgery!

I recall once, at night while in bed, hearing a young woman in an apartment above me clicking her hard heels as she went up the stairs. It made me want to have my walking sound like that. My psychology textbook for my adolescent psychology course had a picture in it of two or three girls talking to a male athlete. One girl wore sling-back white flats. I wanted to wear such shoes.

In two of my classes at CSULB, there was a short young married woman with small feet who had the highest arches I had ever seen on a woman. I envied the shape and size of her feet. She also wore a plaid coat containing yellow, cut on the bias, which I loved. I've always wanted one like it but have never seen one for sale since in either big girl or misses' sizes.

I had to wear a jacket to hide my bust, and my man-tailored clothing was feminine enough in either style or color or both to attract both heterosexual, bisexual, and gay men to me, including one of my university professors who had played football. I was sure he was gay. He even tried to eat lunch with me in the cafeteria. And he gave me an undeserved A grade for the Latin course! But I had no interest in either bisexual or gay men.

About this time, when I ate lunch in the cafeteria for a while, I saw an extremely sissy-looking "boy" there who wore sissy-looking clothes and slippers rather than shoes. As I recall, they were the moccasin or the crisscross over-the-toes sandal type. He seemed very unhappy. I felt sorry for him. I also had a teacher whose palms of his hands were very light and feminine looking, with the backs of his hands being darker, masculine, and hairy. And a "male" accountant in the library had a female rear.

Part III. Living As a Woman

On weekends, holidays, and when alone at home, I would dress up in regular women's dresses, skirts, shoes, and underclothes, plus cosmetics and jewelry. And I would venture out both day and night with a purse, even though I lived in an apartment complex next door to the manager and his son, with his daughter and family across the walkway beyond. Father and son were sometimes in the garage when I walked by down the alley. I watched carefully or turned my head away. And when I met the manager on his bike on the sidewalk one day, he did not show that he recognized me.

In the daytime, I'd go to the park and watch the children, with their mothers, playing. And I wished I were an actual mother. I liked to wear a shiny screen-printed blouse with colorful bubbles on it. Or I'd go to the supermarket, go shopping, or just walk around. One night I took the bus to the First Congregational Church where an organ recital was held. On the way there, a man on the bus said I was beautiful! I also visited the university when school was not in session, and I used the women's restrooms.

At first I wore a wig hat of artificial hair. But it was pulled off by a branch one night on 7th Street, which has a lot of traffic. I turned a corner and walked down a side street toward home. A man drove up, stopped, opened the car door, and asked me where some place was that he indicated, or I associated, with the gay community. I told him the general location where I thought it was. He asked me if I wanted to go with him to show him the way. I said no and walked on. I thought perhaps he had seen my wig fall off!

One day when I was shopping at the May Company wearing my female garb and wig hat, I went into one of the women's departments. The saleslady looked rather shocked when she saw me. I was afraid she had "read" me! Then I went into the ladies' restroom, which had a lounge. I sat down and took off my size 10 B high-heeled white shoes to cool and rest my feet. A lady came in, a saleslady, and sat down beside me.

She talked to me a little, then quickly jumped up and hurried out of the room, faster than I figured she would do to get back to work. I thought she had "read" me—not too good to happen in the restroom! So I hurried out of the lounge myself and took the elevator to a different floor. There was a security guard near the ground-floor elevator doors, but he seemed to pay no special attention to me. His job was to catch shoplifters.

So I let my hair grow long like some of the young men at school were doing, and soon quit wearing the wig hat, which was too warm anyway. When I went to the barber to get my hair cut, he commented on my short hair in front. I said I had trimmed it. So he said I ought not to cut it short in front. (When dressed as a woman, I had bangs to hide my high forehead.) So after that I got my hair cut and styled at the beauticians at Bullock's or the shopping mall while I was dressed in regular women's clothes.

By that time, I had enlarged my bust by using a bust exerciser, from hormone therapy, and my natural female characteristics that encouraged such development. By then I wore man-tailored women's shoes and clothes only at school and in public, except for such things as class observation and student teaching for my teacher-training classes. But on weekends when I was alone, I wore regular women's clothes.

As for instant passability, I let my hair grow long, and wore my man-tailored women's or unisex clothes. So by combing my hair with bangs and carrying a ladies' colorful billfold in my hand, I could go to the post office or store and be called "ma'am" or "miss" okay! Out of habit, some women clerks would say, "Yes, sir!" in answer to a question, or as an exclamation. I didn't like it when it happened, but I didn't let it bother me either.

While I would have preferred to wear a dress or skirt when I wore the above garb, it was okay for the circumstances till I could go full time. But after I went full time, I still wore pants. However, they were more feminine. "I was in heaven!" was how I felt, even when circumstances weren't ideal.

I had also used a homemade clamp I had devised in an attempt at bloodless self-castration. I got the idea from the bloodless surgery method used by farmers and vets on livestock. The job was only partially successful and is *not* to be recommended! This raised my voice somewhat so that when I spoke up in a teacher-training class, I overheard a fellow female student comment to another in class that I would never make a teacher! Today, prescription chemical castration is available. And some sex-reassignment surgery doctors will perform physical castration.

When I went to see Dr. Barbosa, I said something about trying to hide my hermaphroditism. He replied he didn't think I *could* hide it, and he had given enough sex-change operations. I figured he should know! After my bust developed, I had to run to catch the bus at CSULB one day. My breasts were flopping up and down underneath my shirt with no bra; the bus driver was laughing hard when I got on the bus, and I was sure I knew why. And I thought he was my apartment manager's son-in-law!

I looked at men's and women's feet, live or in pictures, when they were sitting down, together or separately, each with a leg over the other knee, and wearing flat shoes. I noticed that the men's feet stuck straight out or upward, whereas the women's feet pointed downward. Also, the women's feet had higher arches and insteps, and they even wore shoe styles to emphasize these facts. I wanted to make my feet more like the females'.

So I sat down on the floor and put my feet under the edge of an armchair with a folded towel over them, then lifted the edge of the chair off the floor with my feet placed just above my toes, then held the chair off the floor till the strain was too much. This stretched the tendons, muscles, and instep skin of my feet so that they began to have more of a female look when I sat down and shortened them in the process by raising my arches and insteps.

When I got used to the weight of the chair, I did as before with my feet under the end of the couch, which was considerably heavier. I did that until it was old hat as well. Two or more times daily I would kneel on the couch or bed with my feet straight back, then I would sit on my heels for several minutes. I also kneeled on the arm of the couch for a short time daily. This all helped to stretch my tendons. Originally, I had been flatfooted. Now I'm not.

Daily at various times, particularly after a bath or shower, and before putting on my shoes, I would bend my feet downward with my hands and hold them down for a time. This helped as above.

Then I read in Dr. Joseph M. Kadans' book, *Encyclopedia of Fruits, Vegetables, Nuts, and Seeds For Healthful Living* (West Nyack, NY, 1973), p. 110, that the organic salicylic acid in grapefruit makes it "one of the most valuable fruits as an aid in the removal or dissolving of organic calcium which may have formed in the cartilage of the joints...." I figured gravity would make much, if not most, of the inorganic calcium, or other inorganic minerals, in the body to settle in the feet. So I started drinking 6 oz. of frozen or canned grapefruit juice once or twice daily, or eating a serving of canned grapefruit sections, hoping this would clean out any inorganic calcium or other deposited minerals in my feet and make them smaller still. About that time I was regularly wearing moccasin shoes. My idea worked. The grapefruit sections seemed to be the most effective.

I also reduced the overall size of my feet, so they would fit better in women's shoes and ultimately a smaller size, by using toenail clippers, preferably the flat-end kind, to cut off the callused skin on my feet, including the thick dead skin on the heels of my feet. Then I used an electric foot sander and ordinary folded rough sandpaper to smooth down the remaining dead skin on my heels. I kept this up for as long as and as often as necessary. I sometimes soaked my feet in water to help.

Ultimately, from doing the above and the feet exercises for *many years* up to the present time, and losing a *lot* of weight, my women's dress shoe size was reduced from a 10 B to a 7½ B, if it has enough toe room! Today I wear a size 7 B casual moccasin shoe. Many years ago, a male designer of women's clothes said on TV that the average size woman's dress shoe at that time was a 7½ B for adult women.

It's very important for me to wear shoes in the smallest sizes possible. I suppose that is because I wasn't allowed to wear feminine girls' shoes as a child. I used to buy girl-style shoes in women's sizes. But they are scarce in the catalogs now, or quite expensive. I guess that's because girls mature earlier than they used to, and so choose women's shoes at an earlier age.

Also, I found that drinking 6 oz. of V-8 vegetable-juice cocktail daily over a period of time reduced the growth of body, facial, and arm/leg hair. If I drank a larger quantity, it seemed also to reduce top-of-head hair, which is a no-no! Eating acid-forming nuts (peanuts, English walnuts, and filberts) helps in the redistribution of my body fat to the skin and bust areas. Also, eating oily foods that are good for the skin (olives, avocados, chocolate, cashews) helps my fat to settle under the skin and lighten it. Starchy foods and ordinary oils deposit fat in large quantities on my body, particularly the abdomen. So I eat them sparingly.

After I developed a bust, I called my sons' attention to it, and told them that God was changing my body. Now I don't believe He had any direct role. And when we went to the store, I carried my woman's billfold in my hand (just like some other women who didn't carry a purse) and asked my boys not to call me "Dad" in public. They both also had begun out of habit calling me "Mom."

And I encouraged this. I told my boys not to tell their mom about me, because she might not let them see me.

When young boys in the neighborhood would see me dressed thus in man-tailored women's clothes and holding a billfold, they would ask me or comment to those with them whether I was a man or a woman. When dressed thus with a billfold in my hand, adults seemed to accept me as a woman and would address me as a woman at the store, post office, shoe repair shop, on the street, etc.

I studied poetry writing at CSULB. So I wrote the following poem when at the university—based upon my research and my experience—but didn't submit it in any poetry course:

TRANSVISION
He saw herself
in the mirror
femininely dressed,
with pink lips,
symbolic jewels,
and shiny tresses.
She smiled through the glass
at his sad, stubbled face
with eyes that leaked
the anguish within.
Yet, he must remain
what she's not.
An electrologist's needle,
a feminizing dose,
a plastic knife, could
change the scene.
But no, without real money
he's left alone,
even by family,
to hack out for herself
a mutilated life
without much hope–
depression, deviled booze,

drugs, suicide–

except for friends, and God.

—*Wendy Phillips, 1967; amended 1996.*

I got my name changed on my credit cards, checks, and utilities, and legally with the state, and later on my disability income. I could change my name in California by adoption without having to go to court or have a lawyer, providing it was not done for illegal purposes. As I recall, I only had to file a form with the state, pay a small fee, and post a notice in a local newspaper. So I posted it in a throwaway paper least likely to be read in my neighborhood.

At first I got a second Social Security card with a new number and my female name. Later, I changed my name on my old card, using a change of name form. When I tried to change my name at the university, they wouldn't do so on the information I gave. I quit soon thereafter. I drove an electric golf-cart type vehicle I had bought from my brother, which required a driver's license. I sold it.

My 10-year-old eldest son saw me pluck hairs from my face with tweezers. So he liked to pluck hairs from my face thus while he sat on my knee—with the excuse that there was nothing better to do. When I put on a dress or skirt and regular women's clothes the last time my boys visited me, I looked and felt like a mother. And when I held them on my lap when dressed thus, I had a feeling of such peace, happiness, and contentment as I had never felt before nor since! The closest to it was many years later when I held a girl around 10 or 11 on my lap in a car. I felt very protective toward her and was prepared to grab her quickly if the car braked suddenly.

I decided it was time to tell my family and ex-wife about my hermaphroditism. I had read an article in the Long Beach Sunday newspaper about Christine Jorgensen, the first known transsexual to receive sex-reassignment surgery, whom I already knew about from my library research. The article said her love life hadn't worked out as she wanted it to. I assumed my ex-wife had seen and read the article, and I called it to her attention. I believe I sent her my copy to be sure she knew about it. She admitted she had read it, but she was still surprised at my revelations about myself. She told me over the phone later that my sexual relations with her had been "all right."

When I informed my family of my hermaphroditism, I told my brother some details first. So I wrote him a letter explaining the fact that I wore women's clothes, and that sometimes when he would stop by my place when he was in Long Beach, I didn't let on that I was home nor let him in because I was dressed in women's clothes. My brother knew my wearing women's clothes was because I was a hermaphrodite of some kind. The next time he dropped by in Long Beach, I let him in even though I was dressed in women's clothes, including shorts. He wouldn't look at me while he talked, which was hard for me to take.

When I wrote the various family members about my hermaphroditism, including this brother again, he told me he told Mother and our eldest brother and others that he thought the members of the family were involved in me being what I was. While they had their part in the matter, I couldn't really agree to any great extent with his idea, as I knew my female sexual status was not basically an acquired status, but an inborn one by inheritance.

Since so many members of my family were educated or had been employed in the health field, I thought they would be more understanding than the medical books said other family members had been before. With both parents as chiropractors, a brother who was also one, a brother-in-law who was an M.D., an uncle who was an M.D., and two sisters who were RNs, plus an aunt and male cousin as nurses, I thought I'd be safe.

So when I wrote them, I was utterly shocked at their response and consternation. I had been told repeatedly throughout much of my life that I was a sissy, pantywaist, crybaby, weakling, tenderfoot, or other such terms that I thought they would be prepared to face the reality of what I am. So I was unprepared emotionally for the opposition I received and their avoidance of me.

After I notified my mother of my real sexual orientation, she mentioned Uncle Paul again, and showed me his picture to show me I didn't need to dress as a woman even if I felt like one. But to me it proved all the more that I did! To whatever extent my female sexuality is inherited, I probably got it from my grandma's branch of the family. Some family members seemed ready to accept me, but then others would interfere.

When I notified my family of my female status mentally, emotionally, and physically, Mother told my elder sister that after they had talked with me about it, she was sure it would all pass away like a nightmare! But all they or anyone else said against my position didn't change a thing. The youngest of my three brothers said that he had felt none of the feelings I had about femaleness, as if his experience should be mine. But it wasn't. A brother-in-law, a school psychologist, wrote me, and had my sister type up his letter (with her admitting having reservations) to say I had disgraced the entire family! Much later, they calmed down enough to visit me once.

My ex-wife consulted a doctor about my case, and he advised her not to let me see my sons anymore, with the argument that they needed a good father figure, which they were already getting via their nice stepfather. She herself felt my boys couldn't have two mothers. Since she had full custody of my sons, I bowed to her wishes; but I never could see any logic in the idea, since because of divorce and remarriage many children have both two mothers and two fathers.

I was so depressed with the situation that I finally gave up my student-teaching program and quit the university. By that time, I had become a skeptic, freethinker, and a libertarian. I moved to Los Angeles and lived and dressed as a woman full time. One reason for moving there was because while shopping in the women's dress department at Sears in Long Beach, I saw a short woman who reminded me of my ex-wife.

Being legally blind and not having seen her for a long time, I wasn't sure. But I figured that eventually we would meet. And I didn't want to meet up with her, given the way she felt about me. The official reason for moving was to write novels and screenplays, which I did, without them being produced or published. Virtually no women's screenplays were produced, anyway!

When I told my landlord I was moving, his daughter and husband said they wanted to measure for carpeting, letting me know when. So just before they came, I took all my female clothes out of the closet and hung them on a clothes-drying rod over the bathtub, carefully closed the shower curtain, then opened the door wide against it. When they came to measure, I stood in the bathroom doorway out of the way, primarily to make sure they didn't use any excuse to enter the bathroom.

Earlier I had sold everything I had–books, bookcase, console stereo, TV, etc.–that I couldn't ship as packages to L.A. on the greyhound bus, check as baggage, or carry with me on Greyhound. I couldn't afford to pay either regular furniture shipping or storage charges on disability income. And I didn't think my eldest brother, who had helped me move to Long Beach, would want to help me move to L.A. as a woman.

When it came time to move, I dressed as female, took the intercity bus to L.A., and checked out apartment ads in the newspaper. Then I went back home after knowing the possibilities in a good part of town. I had the landlord's grandson give my apartment key to his mom or the landlord both of whom were working in another apartment building. Dressed in man-tailored female clothes, I took the city bus to the Greyhound station in the afternoon. In the ladies' restroom in the station, I changed my clothes to more feminine clothes and shoes, and I applied make-up.

Thus dressed I took the Greyhound bus to L.A.. From prior interstate bus travel I was familiar with the Greyhound bus station. I chose it to get to L.A. finally because of its package/ baggage/ luggage-holding facilities, and its lock boxes to hold what I checked out that I couldn't take on a trip on the city bus. In L.A., I took a taxi to a hotel that had a YWCA hotel section and got a room with private bath for one night.

I might have avoided this extra expense. But I wanted the experience of staying in a hotel as a woman! And didn't know when or if I'd ever get the chance again. In the morning, I returned to the Greyhound bus station and put my luggage in a lockbox. Then, via the city bus, I found an apartment I had previously seen advertised. After a few trips on the bus with what I could carry, I finally got all my meager remaining possessions and clothes to my new apartment.

Living full time as a woman was more important to me than having the goods I'd sold, including my expensive console stereo with 15″ speakers I had assembled myself from electronic and cabinet kits! There really wasn't room for it anyway in the bachelorette apartment I rented, which had a desk I needed for writing. Thus, I began my life full time as a woman and notified my family where I was and why. At first, I didn't even have a radio.

When I moved and notified my family of my new address, my eldest sister, a nurse, came to see me. She looked through my clothes hanging in the closet. I was sure it was to see if I had any male clothing. But none was visible, because when I moved, I had put all my male clothing in a bag or suitcase and put it up on the shelf in the closet. I figured my sister would have demanded I wear male clothing if she had seen any! Shortly thereafter, I gave all my male clothing and shoes to the Salvation Army.

When I applied for a job, dressed somewhat fancy, the man who interviewed me asked me over the phone if I had any more clothes. I had very few. I didn't take the job. When I applied for a job at an employment agency, the interviewer asked me if I could pass a medical examination. I said I thought so. He looked at both my ears where I wore clip-on earrings. So I gave up looking for a job and wrote novels and screenplays instead. My mother gave me an old small portable typewriter she had, so I used that for my writing.

I later took more electrolysis treatments at the May Company after I got its credit card. I quit that when the woman working on my underarm hair commented that I needed some work on my face. It cost me too much, anyway. And ever since, I have plucked whatever scant or fine facial hair appeared, and shaved scantily and rarely on my face, and not much or often elsewhere.

I got my hair cut, shaped, or curled in L.A. in the beauty shops at the May Company, Montgomery Ward, and later Penney's. Usually women worked on me, but occasionally a male. I preferred the women. Once I got a permanent at Wards. Some of the chemical got on my right ear and permanently damaged the skin. So I never got another one.

Eventually I let my hair grow as long as it would, curly straight, and only had it trimmed. Now I usually trim it myself. Now it's the longest it has ever been, down below my breasts to my belt in front. In time, its color went from dark brown to brown-blond. As a child, it was blond. For a time I dyed my hair blond. But I got so much male attention I wasn't prepared to deal with, that I quit. The dark brown soon grew out where I parted my hair, anyway.

I not only wanted to live and dress as a woman, but I wanted my family to accept me and thus be able to attend family gatherings as a woman. Because of the rejection I received from some family members, I felt like committing suicide! I would look out the window of my eighth-floor apartment to the parking lot below and think about jumping out the window. But I was held back. Or, when on the stairs, I would look down the open center of the stairwell and think about jumping over the banister to my sure death eight stories below. But I was held back.

When I visited my mother, I came to the front door as did my eldest sister and left the same way. Once at the door when I was leaving, I told my mother I felt like committing suicide. She looked at me for a bit, saying nothing, then replied, "Well, you're doing what you want now." She just didn't understand.

Once when there was a car accident at the nearby corner, and we both went to see it, Mother introduced me as Pauline to her next-door neighbor lady who was also there. Later she said I shouldn't come to the front door when I visited her but walk up the driveway and go into her chiropractic office, which was connected to the back of her house.

Once when I did that, I saw a man I knew come out of the office. When he spoke, I just shook my head and acted as if I didn't know him. Later, when he came back as a patient and told Mother about seeing me and that I looked familiar, she said she told him I was a "very distant" relative. Then she told me she later felt terrible about saying that.

When I started living full time as a female, I went anywhere I wanted to go, day or night, that I could afford. And I went mostly alone. I bought a swimsuit and went to the beach—and experienced guys being interested in me!

I visited very many shopping centers. I dealt with store clerks "as if I owned the place." I researched many libraries. I visited with the people (females) in my eight-story apartment building, both in their apartments and in the lobby. One old man in his nineties got me to go to his apartment on a business deal. But it didn't take long to see he had more than real estate secretarying on his mind! So I left.

I studied photography by home study and bought professional camera equipment and went a lot of places on the bus with it and took a lot of pictures—at the beach, observatory, county fair, museums, around town, skid row. I finally gave up my picture taking, as I had difficulty focusing because of my poor vision. That was before auto-focusing cameras were common or inexpensive.

I went to organ recitals and other music programs. I went to day and evening meetings. Sometimes somewhere I'd meet someone I knew, and they'd give me a ride home. Or they'd see me at a bus stop and give me a ride. Guys would sometimes give me a ride home from church or other meetings. I spoke from the platform and in classes. I tried many things or clothes and shoes once at least just to experience them as female.

I was usually courageous and brave, and when I really wasn't, I acted as if I were! I've done just about anything any well-educated, talented, religious woman would do.

When I rode the bus anywhere, I liked to sit behind the driver and talk to him or her. And they liked to talk to me. Once when I wore hot pink hot pants over pantyhose, a Lions' Club man talked with me at the bus stop at midday and asked me to go for coffee with him. I declined his offer. When I refused, he asked me why I was dressed that way. I said I was going to see my mother.

Another time when I was dressed that way, on the way back home after visiting my mother, I sat behind the black bus driver and talked with him as I often did to drivers. He was really friendly and later invited me to lunch at the end of the line at the bus terminal. I declined him, too.

Part IV. Now and Then

In Long Beach and L.A., I had my picture taken a few times by automatic cameras/developers in drug stores. I did this mainly after getting my hair done.

Mostly, I had no actual problems in being accepted by adults as a woman. Once I got on the bus wearing a women's navy blue Navy pea jacket, and the woman I sat beside said I needed to cut my hair "because I didn't want to look like a girl all my life"! I didn't know for sure what she meant, but it really angered me for a total stranger to tell me how long my hair should be and what I wanted to look like! Especially since she was wrong.

I didn't answer her, so she looked at my feet to see how big my feet were, what shoes I wore, or both. I was sure then I knew what she meant. So I gave the jacket away and decided that in future all my clothes would have colors and designs that were obviously female.

Later, about the time there was something on the news about an Olympic star being a transsexual, I bought a new bike that had the word "Olympic" on the frame. I rode it up to a church in Hollywood to practice the organ. A couple of teen girls on Hollywood Blvd. saw me and said I was a "sex-change." I talked as if I didn't know what they were taking about, in general, and of the star, in particular. But they insisted they knew who and what I was!

When I waited at the bus stops in Hollywood, men would very often stand behind me rather than stand beside me or sit on the bench, as men usually did elsewhere. I figured they were gay men trying to size me up whether I was female. Or that they were women haters.

Eventually I lost enough weight to be lean. So occasionally a boy would ask me if I were a boy or a girl. And I rode a bike a lot to get around. So a few boys and girls of the highly critical junior-high age, talked to me and treated me as if I were one of them! They asked questions or made statements regarding whether I was a boy, girl, or a "he-she," as they put it.

But adults, whether at church, neighbors, businesspersons, or strangers, have said or done nothing to show they had any problem accepting me as female, even when I don't wear visible cosmetics. I'm not as particular in that regard as I once was. The only jewelry I wear has symbolic value—biblical, love-related, and nature-oriented. The Roman cross is an example. Also, I wear love symbols like hearts.

When I used the bus a lot, guys were constantly trying to pick me up at the bus stop, or as I walked along on the sidewalk though I was a total stranger to them! I didn't like this. Many guys would whistle or honk their horns at me. I thought this was flattering and didn't mind. I was not a bathing beauty nor a star. So I was sure they liked the way I dressed.

When I lived in L.A., I recall having at least six transsexuals in my apartment, two individually and four as a group. I also visited another nearby in her apartment. The transsexuals wanted me to be friends with them more than I wanted to be as I wanted to be accepted as 100% female and woman without being reminded of any prior apparent maleness. And I had enough problems of my own that I didn't want to take on others' as well. I failed to realize then that by listening to and helping others with their problems I would help solve and cope with my own.

I also talked on the phone with Virginia Prince, a prominent public crossdresser. She tried to convince me I didn't need and shouldn't even want sex-reassignment surgery—a "hole," as she put it. She didn't convince me in the least!

After writing two screenplays and a novel, I began researching and writing a radical libertarian book. In the fall of 1970, I was about finished with it. Late one afternoon I watched the news on TV about the Jordan civil war in the Middle East. Despite being a skeptic, freethinker, and a libertarian, I was concerned about what was going on there because of my knowledge of Bible prophecy and meditated upon the matter after turning the TV off.

Suddenly I heard an audible "voice" inside my head command me, "Write the book! Write the book!" That was all. I immediately knew what "book" was meant by The Voice because, before I had moved to Long Beach while I was still married, I had contemplated writing a book on Bible prophecy. So the very next day I quit my researching and writing on the libertarian book, and instead began researching for *The Book* in the Los Angeles Public Library.

And the research and writing on *The Book* continues to this day. In researching and writing, I regained my childhood SDA faith and rejoined that church as female by rebaptism in 1974. And my findings for The Book are now published online via AOL and CompuServe in their religion forums. During my continual research for The Book, I heard on the news about transsexuals having female brains. This prompted me to research the Transgender Community Forum. And in the process, I have learned a lot more about transgenderism and gained some nice transgender friends!

In 1971, my ex-wife informed me over the phone that my boys were being adopted and that I shouldn't write to them anymore. She said she had intended to be more lenient with me, but the way my family treated me encouraged her to do the same. Also, her sister had just died. And when I learned of it, I wrote her saying I wished I could visit her sister's husband. That all influenced her attitude. But I hold nothing against her or my family.

I was advised by the adoption agency in Los Angeles to sign my boys over without complaint. If I had taken it to court, I couldn't have won, because of my financial status of living on disability income (because of legal blindness), and to my hermaphrodite status. So I signed my boys away with the understanding they had said they wanted to be adopted by their new stepfather.

Early in L.A. I bought a new electric portable sewing machine, intending to learn how to sew. However, because of my legal blindness, I couldn't get close enough to the needle in the machine to get the thread through the hole. And I didn't see any way to thread the needle otherwise. So I sold the machine at a loss and gave up the idea of sewing. My sewing is now limited to button sewing or re-sewing a small seam with a hand needle.

After I had been living full time as a woman for four years, a male lawyer who had been a classmate of mine organized the 25th anniversary of our graduation from a private religious high school. I didn't go. I had long since lost contact with my classmates. I didn't want to confuse anyone by appearing as female. Neither did I want to dress as male. That was out of the question! I didn't even own any male clothes. And I wasn't about to buy any.

For a time in the mid-1970s, it was the style for women to wear long dresses. So I wore them to church. Early one Saturday morning, while I was standing at the bus stop at Hollywood and Vine to get to the church early to practice the organ for a piece I was to play, a police paddy wagon stopped there and parked. I sensed the cops were watching me. But I had a Bible in my hand and didn't pay any attention to them. And they didn't bother me either and finally drove away before the bus came.

The only real problem I ever had with the cops as a woman was once when I walked across the street on a red light, and a white cop was right there on his motorcycle. He drove across the street after me. When he asked me, I showed him my female ID, and then I explained my poor vision, and he didn't give me a ticket. I even asked him his view on the upcoming election in which the black police chief was running for mayor of L.A.! So we talked awhile.

One day when I researched in the L.A. Public Library, I was wearing pants made of shiny heavy-duty nylon. From a distance, they might have looked like pajamas. At least, a cop must have thought so. When I was standing at the bus stop, he stopped his car out in the street, away from the curb. Then he walked fast on the sidewalk up to where I and a group of other people were standing. He walked through the group and past me on out into the street and back to his car without stopping. Then through the window on the driver's side he talked on his radio (I was sure he was asking about me); then he got in his car and drove off.

Sometimes when I got on or off the bus in downtown L.A. to change buses in what became an extension of skid row, some men would say I was pretty or beautiful. Again, I figured they liked the way I dressed. I figured they didn't see many women in their part of town dressed as I was.

One day when I lived in Pasadena, California, I was standing in line inside the bank. The lady bank manager selected me out of the line over to her desk and gave me first-class preferential treatment with whatever business I was there for. And she offered to do the same for me in the future. I figured she was lesbian. And I didn't think it fair of her to treat me any better than anyone else. So later, after another try or two, she gave up on me.

Since my "basement plumbing" isn't set up for typical male-female sex with me on the bottom, I've remained single since I was divorced, and remain celibate. I'm not really interested in men, anyway.

When my sons became of age at 18, I began to write to each of them again. I hoped they would want to renew our past happy relationship, as we had been very close. But both sons had other interests by that time. It has been slow renewing our former relationship. And it still isn't what I'd like it to be. I still love my sons very much and wish we could be close as we once were.

Once, in a letter, I invited my eldest son to talk to me on the phone. He wrote back that he didn't think he'd want to do that. He said he wanted to remember me as he had known me before. And neither son has offered me his phone number. So, for 27 years, I have not talked to either son on the phone—since my ex-wife prohibited me from seeing them anymore!

I sent my youngest son and my eldest son and his wife much of the information in the expose you are now reading so that they might understand me better. My son's wife had written that her husband had told her all he knew about me. This information, along with some printed material on transsexualism/ hermaphroditism, cleared up some misunderstandings. And my son's wife wrote they appreciated very much the information I had sent.

For a long time she was very faithful in writing to me and sending me cards, till two children came along to take up her time. As of the end of 1995, I had not heard from her in over an entire year, even though I had written several times or sent cards. I love her as a daughter even though I have never seen her. My eldest son wrote occasionally. My youngest son doesn't remember me as well as his brother does, but I heard from him, too. But I've seen neither son in 28 years! Finally, they all quit writing me.

At first, the state of California paid for my estrogen prescription. But when it quit doing so many years ago, I didn't take a hormone prescription anymore. Instead, I ate more cream, and began eating the acid-forming nuts, all of which have phyto (plant) estrogens. I believe that regularly eating cream and acid-forming nuts, particularly peanuts, and avoiding alkaline nuts (almonds), beans (soy), and grain (millet) mostly, handles the initial rise in the pitch of my voice. After its initial rise higher into the alto range, after I partially bloodlessly castrated myself and began taking Premarin.

If my voice had naturally lowered into the bass range, or if I hadn't partially bloodlessly castrated myself, the hormone, cream, and nuts treatment might not have changed the pitch of my voice, nor perhaps its quality. If my mother hadn't raised me up on soybeans and almonds till I left home at age 19, I'm sure I would have developed a bust along with the rest of the secondary female characteristics I developed at the same time girls normally or eventually develop them! Nature really knows best.

Recently a magazine article for girls called my attention to one difference between boys and girls. While boys' voices change abruptly so that it changes between high and low beyond the boys' control, girls' voices lower in pitch gradually so there is no noticeable change. I do not recall my voice ever changing abruptly like boys' voices do, but gradually like girls' voices. And even then it didn't lower naturally (temporarily) below the tenor range (bass B flat-middle G). For a while after marriage, I forced my voice down to bass F. But when I quit that, my voice gradually returned to the tenor range, and eventually to the alto range, which is natural for me.

Now for many years my voice has risen and remained higher so that it was in the lower and middle portion of the untrained contralto (alto) range (tenor F-soprano D). For some time, with no falsetto, I could sing middle A 440 Hz., and sometimes B flat in the treble clef. In January 1996, after I daily applied Cortaid to my throat morning and evening for about two weeks, my voice rose a 4th so that I could softly sing soprano D!

I could then sing tenor F. And when I answered the phone, my voice sounded higher than before I used the Cortaid on my throat. Having this natural female range for many years helps to account for my voice, and for being accepted as female. It will be interesting to see how much higher my voice will rise at either or both ends of the female-voice spectrum. As of 2/2/96, I could weakly sing soprano D sharp! And as of 8/21/98 I could comfortably sing tenor G.

Cortaid contains 1% hydrocortisone, a hormone of the adrenal cortex derived from cortisone, a steroid hormone of the adrenal cortex. Both hormones are used similarly. "Female pseudohermaphrodites are genetically females, but their genitals have been masculinized through a malfunction of the adrenal gland known as the congenital adrenogenital syndrome." (Bibliography: Jones, Howard W., and Scott, William W., *Hermaphroditism,*

Genital Anomalies, and Related Endocrine Disorders, 2d ed. (1971); Van Niekerk, Willem A., True Hermaphroditism (1974). *Grolier's Academia American Encyclopedia*–1994)

When my favorite brother died, I decided that whatever scraps mentally and physically were left of "Paul" had died and were buried with him in his grave! I had been one of his pallbearers, and I determined I would never be one again. Since that time, I have not responded to the name "Paul" in person, over the phone, or by mail. No such person lives at my address. If I recognize the caller's voice, I let them talk; otherwise I hang up.

I wanted to change my first name from "Paul" to "Frances," but decided on "Pauline" instead for my family's sake, particularly my mother's, who named me at birth. I changed my middle name from "Welcome" to "Wendy," which neither my mother nor other family had to deal with. My name is "Pauline" by legal adoption, and that is the only first name I go by for any purpose. And I also changed my middle name by adoption. I never liked my middle name anyway and see nothing female about it. I prefer to be addressed as Wendy—as it has no connection to my birth name, and because I chose it myself. But I use both names, depending on the circumstances.

After Mother moved into a mobile home, she once introduced me to one of her neighbors when we went out to the trash bin. I later saw a lot of what I suspected were my dead brother's women's clothes hanging in a closet. When I commented about them, Mother offered them to me, but I declined to take any of them. They were too sexy for my taste, and I didn't want to wear anything that reminded me of my brother in that way.

After most of my family rejected me in my female-hermaphrodite role, I was no longer invited to attend any family gatherings at Thanksgiving, Christmas, etc. It was a lonely time on such days for many years, as long as I was in city-bus traveling range to them. That is the one reason I moved to Missouri to be away from them.

When Mother died, I wasn't able to go to her funeral because my eldest brother said an unnamed member of the family refused to attend if I were there. So I dressed up as if I were going to the funeral and went to the public library that day instead. Truly, I'm a woman "of sorrows, and acquainted with grief"!

My elder sister wrote me afterward saying she saw nothing feminine about me in activities, looks, or outlook. She said she believed I would look, feel, and live better as a male. She didn't think building an organ was a female activity. (I had invented, designed, and built an electronic organ that would play in just intonation.) Family members believe what they want to believe!

At least she admitted she might be wrong, and included some sisterly advice on dress, etc. Later she sent me an illustrated article *from The Pueblo Star Journal and Sunday Chieftain*, Pueblo, CO, Sunday, 1/9/1983, page 2B, entitled "Billy Cox: A prisoner in his own body." She said she sympathized with me after reading it and reading what I had written.

Beginning some years past and for several years I studied for therapy magazines (*'Teen, Seventeen, Sassy, YM*) and books intended for girls ages 10-19, so that I would learn the truth about girls' interests, emotions, hopes and dreams, attitudes toward girls and boys, and the attitudes of boys toward girls. I also read *Madamoiselle* for unmarried young women.

This all has been a real eye opener and has verified what I have said all along—that I am 100% female psychologically. I identify 100% with girls or women on almost everything—except what I consider their "nonsense" about the *latest* fashions in clothes, cosmetics, and jewelry, or any immoral ideas. I have found no accurate likeness between me and boys or men psychologically, and hardly anything physically.

There was enough aggressive romance in me at one time to chase after a girl and ask her to marry me. But after I married her, I either didn't know what to do with her, or lacked sufficient incentive to do what I knew from a male perspective! I had no problem with general romance—hugging, kissing, holding, cuddling. But giving flowers and being very intimate, as if I were male, were problems.

I wanted to dress and be treated as a woman, a wife, not treat a woman from a husband's perspective. And I didn't want to be the decision-maker of the home on many things. I didn't really want to be a husband (house-band). I felt more like I needed someone to take care of *me*—rather than me take care of her. Especially since I was legally blind.

Once at a party while we were eating, a man asked me if he could dance with my wife; I said it was up to her. So he asked, and she complied. Later she said she hadn't really wanted to dance with him.

I also read Harlequin romance novels available in the public library or by mail. One newsletter accompanying the books I got by mail said some of these novels have been used by counselors of men who have problems relating to women or to their own wives. I figured reading some of these books could help me tell if I identified mostly or fully with the hero or heroine. If I identified myself with the heroine, I was surely a female hermaphrodite, I decided. And I identified with the woman in all the stories, virtually 100%! And never with the man.

After becoming bony-lean in build, I still had a female spine curvature with female hips, waist, and rear. My height was thus reduced from 5′ 11½″ to 5′ 9″. I weighed as low as 111 lbs. As of 8/21/98 my body measurements were 36″ bust, 27″ waist, and 39″ hips. I wore a 32 C bra. When I weighed + or – 115 lbs., there was a spring and lightness in my step–like a girl's–that is missing when I weigh a lot more. So I much preferred to be light in weight. I could wear smaller clothes that way besides. But I looked better at the 136 lbs. I weighed. As of 2/2/99 I weighed 150 lbs. and needed a 36 D bra.

Some say that when a woman sits up straight in a chair, a cat should be able to crawl between her back and the chair back. This is because the typical female has a protruding rear. And a cat can crawl between my back and a chair back when I sit up straight!

I wore a size 6 or even smaller in Misses dress. Originally I wore Tall sizes but have not for many years. The regular Misses, or even Petite sizes with a crumpled waist, fit me better. The clothes designer mentioned earlier had said the average women's dress size then was size 14. I prefer clothing of floral, fruit, hearts, or cats design in preference to solid colors.

Because of my petite horizontal build I can wear some clothes in big-girl sizes, and I do. They're usually not only cheaper than Misses sizes, but most of the cute clothing is now only made for girls since most women work outside the home. But I can remember when more women stayed home, and their clothes were much cuter then than they are now.

The physical size of the clothes I wear is very important to me—the smaller the better that will fit! I guess that is because I wasn't allowed to wear feminine girls' clothes as a child. So fortunately my wishes in that regard can be fulfilled. Both sexes of all ages have expressed appreciation for my clothing and shoe choices in color or design.

I saw advertised a "Personal At Home Ear Piercer," with 14KT gold ball earrings included, by Inverness. With it one could pierce a child's, a friend's, or one's own ears. It was advertised as 100% safe and 100% sterile. I bought it from Sears and pierced my own ears. Being legally blind, I didn't do a perfect job. I knew some beauticians pierce ears for a reasonable sum, and that some M.D.'s pierce ears for a higher fee. The reason I pierced my own ears was mainly because I had heard of the possibility of one getting AIDS from the process when done with ear piercers that had been used before and not properly sterilized!

Once a few years ago I wasn't careful enough when taking off my top, and actually tore my earring from my left ear, leaving a tear in the lobe. Today the tear isn't nearly as long as it once was. So hopefully in time most or all the tear will disappear. Ear tissue grows slowly.

I see the difference between sleeping as a woman and as a man is that a woman will normally dream dreams in which she is a woman, whereas a man will normally dream dreams in which he is a man. A transgender may have a combination of the two. Now (in 1999) in my dreams I am a woman, with female romantic ideas. If I'm interested in a woman in my dream, or her with me, I may call her attention to the fact that I'm a woman. However, it's natural for me, as a hermaphrodite, to be interested in females. Especially after being lovingly married to one for eight years.

After many years, my only living brother, a chiropractor, and his wife contacted me only when our eldest brother died. My youngest and favorite sister, whom I played with very much as a child, and later went around town with, is a nurse married to an M.D.; she has completely rejected me. I've sent her many cards and letters throughout the years, and she never responds. Once I sent her pictures I had taken of our mother and sisters, and she sent them back without explanation. I write occasionally to my ex-wife, whom I still love in the back of my mind, but she never answers either.

I think my crossdresser brother's and my cases are both part of our inheritance from our grandma's branch of the family which very sissy Uncle Paul came from and whom I discussed earlier. This inheritance may account in part for why our eldest brother never married even though he was a normal man.

My youngest brother had asked his wife to do things which she thought he, as the man of the family, should do and not use his poor vision as an excuse not to do. I did similarly when married and used my poor vision as the excuse.

So perhaps his behavior in that regard may likewise be traceable to Grandma's branch of the family. He told me he was free from any female characteristics, but one's inheritance affects one's behavior.

When I sent my siblings the original copy of this discussion, my two living brothers, my youngest sister, and my sister-in-law did not respond. My eldest sister, an R.N., called me on the phone, saying she had already studied all about the matter at the university, and that there was nothing I could tell her about it that she didn't already know.

She still called me by my birth name till I insisted she not do so. I recall her saying she threw my discussion of myself or of my crossdresser brother or both into the wastebasket, saying I was not to send any more stuff like that! Then later, when I sent her two news releases about transsexual brains being female, she wrote back that she already utterly knew all about the subject long ago.

Eventually my psychologist brother-in-law, who is married to my elder sister, and I were fully reconciled. He wrote me to that effect and once came to visit me over the weekend on a trip he was taking. We talked a lot. He said he, as a psychologist in a public school system, had learned a lot about sexually related problems. I considered him a genuine friend when he left!

Despite my poor vision and partial colorblindness, I have a sense of and appreciation for beauty. So now I'm attracted to pretty women who are younger than me. But since I'm an intersexual, I've never admitted to myself or others than I'm lesbian. I have no adequate explanation for my feeling. And they've never been strong enough toward males to consider me as bisexual.

For a time I was attracted to handsome men. But did nothing about it because my "basement plumbing" is not in proper working order for that! So being safe, I befriended married men at church or as neighbors whom I had reason to believe wouldn't be any threat to either me or their families.

I once had a crush on a young engineer who lived next door to me in the apartment building. He got a new car soon after he started work here at Chance. I made a fool of myself by writing notes to him and posting them on his door. His girlfriend or new wife moved in with him, and then they moved away. I felt bad both about learning he had a girlfriend/wife and about him moving away. I hardly ever think about him anymore now. So it wasn't anything really serious. I was reading romance novels and I figure that had a lot to do with what I did and felt.

Because of a skin-infection problem some years ago I regularly applied Cortaid cream to my skin. It made the hair on my arms, legs, and pubic area grow more sparse, finer, shorter, and lighter, except for a few stragglers.

More recently I began to apply Cortaid daily to my scrotum and penis area, as I had done before to my throat. It softened and shrunk my scrotal/penis skin and softened and reduced the size of my testes and small penis to almost nothing! It also reduced hair growth more both in the groin/pubic area and on my face. I still pluck a few hairs now and then. But there's virtually little need to shave!

This treatment, particularly along with the application to my throat, put more fat on my lean face, making it look younger and more feminine. At first it also made me want to flirt with the men at the post office, hardware store, and supermarket the next time I went to town. Nothing sexy, just friendly—to make them smile, chuckle, or laugh. I felt more like a woman than I had in a long time! But in time, that died away.

In the women's panties/briefs section of a large mail-order catalog such as Penney's, you can see that many of the women models have some protrusion in the vaginal area. Now my protrusion is no more than theirs, and generally less when wearing panties!

A few years back, as mentioned, I tore an earring from my left ear. So I wore only one earring for quite some time. While walking in the park, a teen boy drove by. I overheard him tell his girlfriend I looked like a transsexual. The word got around. And when I met kids of varying ages who went to the park, some would ask questions about my sexual status. I tried to ignore them all as much as possible.

Once, when riding my bike, two boys followed me home on their bikes and carried on foolishly. Some girls learned where I live. They came by several times on their bikes and later in a car, banging on my door and asking questions. One girl even took my picture! Later they started coming by at night around midnight, once even later, banging on my door or window, and calling my name or asking questions, or making remarks.

Most of the kids who gave me a hard time seemed to live on the "wrong" side of the tracks. They didn't have enough money to do much other than get into trouble or bother people. I once rode my bike through that part of town to the SDA Community Center that provides food and clothing for those in need, to give them my clothes and shoes that were in good condition but which I no longer wanted. Several elementary boys on bikes gave me a hard time by asking sex questions and making crude remarks. One asked me if I had a "whistle."

In the light of the above, my physical characteristics, and my latest research, I realize I'm more than merely what some would call a transsexual psychologically, or even physically. My condition is also fully biological. I have a female brain. I'm a 100% female-oriented hermaphrodite or a female pseudohermaphrodite. There's no doubt in my mind about this! The exact definition is immaterial since both are genetically female.

I am what nature made me to be, and of myself I can be nothing else. And naturally, I have *no desire* whatever to be male, any more than a typical genetic female would. I'm only following as best I can the medical treatment prescribed for such persons as myself to the extent I have knowledge, opportunity and can afford, rather than commit suicide as many in the transsexual class have done, especially those who can get no help, have no friends, or have no hold on God.

Those who get help can be constructive citizens and contribute to society, and to a church if they are religious. Without such help they may seem to be virtually useless to themselves or to the world after their problem manifests itself in all its force. And it grows on a transsexual or hermaphrodite mentally, and very often physically–just as a girl, even a tomboy, gradually matures into womanhood.

Sequel: My Younger Son

My younger son, Jon (Jonathan), adopted by his stepfather, and whom I hadn't seen in 30 years since he was 8 years old, who was on business at a trade show in Kansas City for Shopsmith, rented a car there, and drove around 150 miles to Centralia, Missouri, to visit me today!

He had called Saturday night after I was in bed to work out the details. He called again Sunday to say his plans were still on. Then called earlier today saying he was leaving Columbia.

We had a delightful visit. He said his original plan for some time had been to have both he and my elder son, Tim (Timothy), visit me, but that it had never worked out geographically. And that he would tell Tim he has visited me.

I told him why I was not allowed to see him or Tim. Because my ex had consulted a psychiatrist who said they needed a father figure, and that I, a female intersexual, shouldn't be allowed to see them anymore.

Then he invited to take me out to dinner rather than me having to prepare lunch for him. I didn't know the best place to go. So we checked out several places in town and ended up in Pizza Hut. He treated me like a lady by holding the doors for me, paying the bill, and unlocking the right-side car door and opening it for me.

Later, he drove back to catch his plane to Idaho.

For several years, I thought Jon had rejected me after he quit writing me. But he said he was busy with his new business. And all he really needed to want to visit me was time to both accept me as I am and see me that way. He commented that must be the reason he failed to contact me when I lived in Pasadena, California, after he became an adult. For he admitted he had felt lost for several years after he was no longer allowed to see me—because we had been so close.

I'm very proud of Jon. For a son who was adopted against my will to spend so much money and time on me when he doesn't profess to be religious means a very great deal to me!

As a small boy, he went into the bathroom and asked Jesus to come into his heart. I think He did! To make room in his heart for Jesus, he thought he had to get rid of something inside. He had the right idea in principle.

So I'd say whether G, L, B, T, or I, who want acceptance by someone, don't give up or lose hope, but be patient and pray! We didn't discuss any gay or lesbian issues specifically because he didn't ask. Other than asking how I became acquainted with and friends with Sara, whose pic he saw. He referred to my intersexual role change as a choice, but I chose not to say more about it.

Remember, that for many people to accept a transsexual or an intersexual who changes from the sex-gender role assigned at birth is harder than accepting someone who's "merely" GLB! Even some GLBs seem to have a problem with it.

Copyright 1996, 1998, 1999 by Wendy Phillips
Pauline Wendy Phillips was an intersex Seventh-day Adventist who was living in the Midwest at the time of writing this story.

UPDATE[1]: Wendy passed away in September 2017. Wendy was a resident of Washington at the time of passing.

---

1. *https://www.legacy.com/obituaries/name/wendy-phillips-obituary?pid=186678171*

Finding Peace

By David Coltheart

I was born in New Zealand into a good Adventist home—my father was the conference evangelist and my godly mother his most faithful assistant. We moved house every year and then, when I was 9, we were transferred to Australia. Three years later, my dad baptized me at the evangelistic meeting he was conducting. But even at that age, I knew there were certain things that triggered my mind and I always felt guilty about them.

I never enjoyed sporting activities since I preferred to read a book rather than get rough and dirty. Despite that, I had some good friends in my class at the Adventist high school and I got along well with them. But my best friend was different. The other boys teased him, and I couldn't figure out why. All I knew was that there was something that drew me to him, something that no one talked about.

When I was 14, we moved to London. I knew there was something different about me I couldn't define. Sex was not discussed at home or at the Adventist school in England where I spent my teenage years and I remained in questioning ignorance. I was an excellent student and did well academically. But when I wasn't immersed in studying, I secretly admired a fellow student who was a keen sports person, socially confident and good-looking.

The word "gay" wasn't used in the late 1960s. The only word, whispered in shocked undertones, was "homosexual"—and I knew I wasn't one of them. But when I was 17, I was accused of being a "homosexual" because I didn't play football and never had girlfriends. The abusive word stung, and I hotly denied the charge—there was nothing in my life even to suggest that I fitted the stereotype. The confrontation passed, but my identity was in question. Was it true, I wondered? Did someone know more about me than I knew myself?

Answering what I still believe was a call from God, I studied for the ministry at Newbold College. Like everyone else, I dated girls, but the occasions were scary and awkward. I was always relieved when the event was over. I became friends with a student from Eastern Europe who expressed his feelings more openly than I did. Sometimes he innocently put his hand on my shoulder or gave me a manly hug. My heart beat faster, but the moment passed, and I never said a word. The next summer, both 19 years old, we worked together selling children's books door to door. I longed for a closer relationship—but I kept my dreams to myself.

After three years at college, I volunteered as a student missionary and enjoyed the adventure of travel and the challenge of evangelism in West Africa. While there, I wrote to a girl I knew from college, but the romance crashed and I was relieved. I had always preferred the company of male friends, anyway. But I was troubled. Did God condemn me for something that was not my fault and had always been a part of me since early adolescence? I carried a burden of guilt that prayer and Bible study could not erase.

I completed my master's degree at Andrews University. About that time, my father died and our family returned to Australia. I started my work in public evangelism, a role I knew was God's will for my life. I assumed one day I would fall in love, marry, establish a home, and live happily ever after. That was what my church decreed, society required, and my family expected. I believed marriage would "fix the problem." But even after I met someone and became engaged, I didn't "feel" romantic and wasn't sure I was doing the right thing. Since I didn't dare trust anyone with my secret, I decided it was better to say nothing and hope for the best. After the wedding, I knew I had done the right thing—I had passed into a society where everyone was nicely arranged in pairs. Because everyone approved of what we had done, I assumed I was in love.

As conference (and later union) evangelist, my wife and I moved 12 times over the next 20 years. Every shift was a fresh start, and I determined, with God's help to conquer my desires by sheer willpower. I read the Bible, looking for answers, and I prayed God would change me. But the formula never worked for me. My prayers, though answered in every other way, on this subject were unanswered. I knew my church disapproved and my conscience troubled me. Not only was homosexuality a sin, but it was also an "abomination." While other sins were preached about, this sin was never even whispered, let alone discussed. By implication, this made it the worst of all sins, reinforced by instant loss of membership, followed by ostracism and separation from church life. Was it so bad to be unforgivable?

I was in a quandary. I loved my job, but apart from theology degree, I had no other skill or training and apart from the church, there was nowhere else to go. I was desperately afraid for my identity and my livelihood. As the sole wage earner, I had a family that included three sons to care for. I wanted to talk to someone. At church meetings and ministerial retreats, I scanned everyone I met, hoping to find someone to whom I could confide. But to even breathe the slightest hint of my problem was to invite exposure. There was no one in the church I trusted. I reacted with anger and frustration, taking out on those I loved my inability to find peace of mind—but in solitude I wept. I stared into the depths of a black hole from which there seemed no escape.

My belief in God's grace never wavered and my assurance of personal salvation was never in doubt, but while attending a camp meeting, I experienced a new conversion. After nights of tears and repentance, my days were suddenly filled with joy and hope. Despite my feelings, God still accepted me, still loved me. At the end of that week, in the silence of a beautiful bush setting, a fellow minister baptized me in a nearby stream. He knew of my experience though not the struggle behind it. That Sabbath morning was the most precious moment of my entire life, before or since. I even dared to hope that my problem was cured.

It was not to be. Although the commitment remained, and the glory of my decision has never left me, my basic nature was unchanged. I was not wrestling with a mere problem, but a deep, inner mindset that was beyond choice. I seemed to be always going against the grain, locked in a grim struggle between me and a world that refused to acknowledge such feelings existed. The thought of being a gay Adventist minister was too horrifying to contemplate, and I buried the problem under a mountain of guilt and despair. Since I couldn't fix the problem, then I had to stand it.

After praying for months for a change of direction, I accepted the task of editing a magazine for an independent ministry supportive of the church. The next five years were the happiest and busiest of my life, and my life took new directions. More importantly, I gained new skills.

About that time, we connected to the internet. I typed in the words "gay" and "Adventist" and to my astonishment, discovered SDA Kinship. I discovered I was not alone after all. Suddenly, I could identify with something tangible. And there were people who affirmed my life and experience. But it still took years before I came out of denial. It happened when I looked in the mirror one morning and said, out loud, "You're gay." I couldn't believe what I had said, but the realization had been creeping up on me for years. Acceptance came slowly and now all that remained was to tell someone.

I grew up in an era when Adventists didn't go to the movies, so I felt awfully guilty when I sneaked out to see *Brokeback Mountain*. That was the turning point. As the achingly beautiful story unfolded, I knew it was my story. I was overwhelmed by a tsunami of emotion and tears. Now the pain of staying in was worse than the pain of coming out, and I figured I only had a few months to plan my exit strategy. I set a date to tell my wife and family and made my preparations. I had been practicing my speech for years, but now it became an obsession. On the appointed day, I still hesitated, right until the last second, knowing that civilization was about to end. I drew a breath, and to my astonishment, told my story.

I woke next morning to a day I never expected to see. I felt as if the burden of my life had rolled away and the relief was palpable and real. I had already written a letter of resignation to my beloved church—now I gave it to the church pastor. Events outside my control took over and after almost 30 years of marriage, I moved out of the family home, bought a fridge and a microwave and began living alone.

As the process of self-disclosure continued, I had to surrender my job and, for the first time, I was unemployed. For months, things got steadily worse, and I felt as if I was falling down a deep pit without reaching the bottom. When it was obvious there were no jobs for me in the local area, I packed up my few possessions, rented a small truck and shifted 1000 kilometers north to Queensland. I still had nowhere to go, but that's when God intervened.

By a series of apparently random circumstances, I shared a house with a man on the north side of Brisbane. More coincidences followed over the next couple of months, which led me to a job as a technical writer for a training organization in a semi-rural area 100 kilometers north of the city. I rented a flat on the same day and suddenly the darkness was over. I found a small, welcoming church to attend and a circle of church friends who knew my story and accepted me, regardless. Looking back, I realize the random circumstances were not mere coincidences, but a series of remarkable providences, each one linked to the next, by which God led me to where I am today.

Six months later, I bought a house near where I work. I live in a beautiful area surrounded by rainforest, close to the beach. I have some great friends and a supportive family. I praise God for His love and grace. He has led me all the way, and I thank Him for His blessings. I can only look back and see His providential hand over me, guiding me and caring for me. Now my faith is stronger than ever. My spiritual life is deeper and more meaningful. Most of all, I have peace of mind knowing that He accepts me and loves me.

David Coltheart lived on the Sunshine Coast in Australia, at the time of this writing, where he attended his local Seventh-day Adventist Church. He enjoys bushwalking, going to the beach, and making new friends. Currently (2016) he has written and published his 300-page autobiography, Finding Out, *available at http://findingout.webs.com/.*

Flight to Kampmeeting

By Gary K. Stebbeds

It happened on the trip to my first Kampmeeting—the second Kampmeeting of Kinship. I could not attend the first one.

Two of the women that I worked with at the phone company kept bugging me until I sent in my reservation, and they paid for my cost of Kampmeeting that year. Then they kept on me until I purchased my plane ticket. When it came time to go to the airport, they asked our boss if they could go to the airport to see me off, as I had no family to go with me. He said sure. They came to make sure I got on the plane. They knew about my being gay, and that the Kampmeeting was a GLBTI event. They also felt that I had to go, and they made sure that I was on my way.

This was when President Reagan had fired the air controllers. My flight left Rhinelander, Wisconsin, for Green Bay, Wisconsin. I changed planes there, and flew to Milwaukee, Wisconsin. Changed planes again and flew to Las Vegas. On the leg to Las Vegas, we were zig-zagging through the desert, trying to avoid this in air flight, and that one. It was a real mess.

It was on this portion of the flight that I started having a real guilt trip about my being gay, remembering what I had been taught from my earliest memories. I was convinced that I was wrong, and needed to change, and here I was going to a GLBTI Kampmeeting. I was trying to study my Bible, couldn't concentrate on it, and so I silently prayed that since I was in a saved relationship and that if by going any further, I would be wrong and lose my salvation, I asked God to end my life. Crash the plane, give me a heart attack, whatever it took to end my life. Or give me assurance that being gay was okay and to also give me some peace.

It was at that moment that what felt like an electrical shock started at my head, went through my entire body, and out through my feet—and such a peace came over me. I had never had such a wonderful feeling of peace prior to that time, nor since. At that point, I knew it was in God's plan that it is okay to be gay, as this is how I am made, and it is God's plan for me. I would like to add, that anyone who says that it is not okay is going against God's will.

Gary K. Stebbeds is his real name.

Full Circle

By Jan Radclyffe

The first person I ever truly fell in love with was a Catholic woman, whom I met in college; Kari was a freshman when I was a senior. After she graduated and finished her internship, we got an apartment together. I was 23 when we had our first sexual experience, which just seemed to happen naturally in the course of the intimate friendship we had developed. We lived together for five years, but internalized homophobia from our religious upbringings wouldn't allow us to accept our sexuality. Although we were lovers in every sense of the word, we denied—even to ourselves—that we were lesbians. We told ourselves we were simply two people who fell in love with each other—and both just happened to be female! (It was easier to admit that I loved "a woman," than to admit that I loved "women"—or that I loved her *because* she was a woman.) We told other people we were roommates and best friends, which were both true. We lived far enough away from both of our jobs that no one really had a clue about our private life. We weren't living as "out" lesbians—we didn't go to bars (straight or gay) or even find a support group. We just worked, attended concerts, flew kites, took trips together, and totally enjoyed being in love with each other. She often attended church with me on Sabbath mornings, and I sometimes attended mass with her on Sunday mornings.

Three and a half years later, Kari's co-worker arranged a small dinner party to introduce Kari to one of her husband's friends. Keith was really nice, and Kari quickly fell in love with him. It was kind of painful when she would go out with him and then come home and tell me all the intimate details, but at least she was still sharing intimacy with me. Later on, he began spending weekends at our apartment, and I got to listen to them making love in the room next to mine—ouch! They were married two years after their first meeting. People are expected to cry at weddings, so no one suspected that the tears in the maid of honor's eyes were a mixture of "happy for my friend" tears and "my heart is broken" tears.

I had to reassure myself that the same thing could happen to me. Before they were married, Keith had set up a blind date for me with one of his friends. Joel and I dated for over two years and had a lot of fun. I admired him for having high moral standards; even though we were in our late twenties, he never tried to be sexually intimate with me. (That's probably why I went out with him for so long.) When he was sent to the Philippines for a year, he told me not to sit around waiting for him. He said he had a lot of "personal issues"—such as his religion—that he had to resolve within himself, before he'd be ready for a serious relationship with anyone. So we parted as friends. (We ran into each other at a gay Halloween celebration more than ten years later and came out to each other!)

After Joel left, I met a nice Adventist man at an Adventist Singles retreat. Ed had just gotten a new job in another state, so we "dated" by letter and by phone and saw each other once every six months—which made the relationship always seem new and exciting. He was attracted to me, so I told myself that this might be my last chance to get married and let God change me. I guess I allowed myself to fall in love with the idea that he loved and cared for me. We both knew that intercourse was a "no-no" before marriage, but that didn't stop us from doing everything short of it. And since the things we did felt good to me, I was convinced that this was God's answer to my prayers. When Ed asked me to marry him, I was 32 years old and figured and that marriage would be my salvation from being attracted to women. (After all, we were taught that if we asked God to take away "unnatural desires," S/He would do so.)

What a let-down my wedding night was. Even though we "became one flesh," the feeling of emotional fulfillment—the incredible sense of oneness—I had experienced with Kari was totally absent. After Ed rolled over and began snoring, I cried myself to sleep. I had just left a great job and lifelong friends that I loved, and I had committed to moving across the country to a place where I had no friends. But the most empty feeling came from knowing I had promised myself to this man for the rest of our lives—in a marriage that should never have taken place.

During the seven years of our marriage, I gave God every chance to strike me straight make me feel fulfilled in my marriage, but it didn't happen. I was extremely lonely and had a lot of time on my hands, because Ed worked overtime, took night classes, and went away on frequent business trips. We bought a VCR, and I rented a lot of movies. It was when I watched *Personal Best* that a light went on inside my head and forced me to admit to myself that I was still attracted to women. The movie is about two female athletes training for the Olympics, who fall in love and begin a long-term relationship. Of course, filmmakers thought they could only make a movie about lesbians if one becomes straight or kills herself at the end, so in *Personal Best* one of them falls in love with a guy. (I could really identify with the *other* one's feelings!) At the end of the movie, the two of them are on the victory stand together, and the boyfriend is standing nearby, cheering. His girlfriend whispers to her former lover, to ask what she thinks of him. When Tory whispers back, "He's kinda cute—for a guy!", I realized she *didn't* automatically assume that she, too, now had to find a guy. I knew I'd been aroused by watching the love scene and all the female athletes' bodies, but it was that closing scene which helped me realize that even though Ed was "kinda cute—for a guy," I needed a deep emotional bond with a woman to make me happy.

For the first time, at age 38, I admitted to myself that I'm a lesbian. That felt both liberating and terrifying at the same time. It felt good to finally admit the truth to myself, after all those years of living in denial. But I also felt like it would cost me my salvation, as well as my marriage, if I acted upon my newfound identity. I was convinced that I would have to live a life of suppressing my true nature and honor the marriage vows that I had made before God and family. But I got curious and browsed the "Gay & Lesbian Studies" section in a big bookstore downtown. Through a listing in *Yellow Pages* and a classified ad in MS. magazine, I learned of the existence of Kinship. I rented a P.O. box and began receiving their materials. It was a great relief to learn that nowhere in the Bible or the Spirit of Prophecy is there a mention—let alone a condemnation—of homosexuality as one's natural orientation.

After a lot of prayer and soul-searching, I realized it wasn't fair to Ed, or to myself, to continue in the marriage—and that God would forgive me for breaking a promise I had made under a false assumption. When I left him, I told Ed he deserved someone who could love him in return, as much as he loved her. I never told him—or anyone in the church—that I was gay. Going through a divorce was a heart-wrenching experience for both of us, and I felt like a failure to my family.

The Adventist church where Ed was still a member refused to transfer my membership to the church where I moved. They said the Holy Spirit impressed them I was no longer a member in good and regular standing, and my name was removed from the church books. To someone who had: attended Sabbath School from birth, gone to Adventist schools from first grade through college, taught in church schools for twelve years, and led the Primary Sabbath School division for three years, that was like having the rug pulled right out from under me. I was left flat on my back, gasping for breath like Charlie Brown when Lucy moves the football before he can kick it. I got the message that to begin my new identity as a lesbian, I had to give up my old identity as an Adventist.

Fortunately, God didn't abandon me, even though the SDA church did. Thanks to Kinship, I learned the truth that God accepts and loves me as I am—and that I was never meant to live the lie of heterosexual marriage. On the surface, it's possible to fool people into thinking, "What a perfect couple," because they can't see the emptiness in your soul. But no one should have to live like that. I've come to be very thankful that God will be the only judge of who will and who won't be in heaven. Despite the church's official opinion, there are two things I've always been—and always will be: a Seventh-day Adventist and a lesbian! Through Kinship, I've formed lifelong friendships and met my life partner. Only God knows what Her/His plan is for the rest of my life. I've learned to say, "Thy will be done" and accept it—one day at a time!

Jan Radclyffe is a closeted, partnered Seventh-day Adventist lesbian who has been married to a man, but has come full circle back to loving a woman.

Growing Up Gay SDA

By Ronald Lawson

This Christmas was going to be different. As usual, I attended the junior camp run by our local conference. But this year, because I was so "mature" for a nearly 14-year-old, I could stay on for the youth camp that followed. The night between the two camps, Peter moved into my dorm.

I had known him at a church during the time we lived on a pineapple farm in Queensland. We had moved there from my birthplace in Sydney, Australia, when I was six years old. Then, when I was eleven, we moved to Toowoomba, a provincial "city" of 40,000. That was because Dad had allowed himself to be talked into becoming a literature evangelist. This was but one sign I grew up in the bosom of the church. Dad seemed to be elected elder wherever we went, and he was on the conference executive committee for years. "Mum" had taught in Adventist colleges in India and Australia before marriage. We also had a relative in high places in the church hierarchy.

I remember realizing that I was different when I was about five years old. I didn't have a name for it yet, of course, nor was it expressed yet in sexual attraction. Perhaps it was feeling more comfortable with girls than boys, not liking the rough and tumble of boy behavior; perhaps it was my love for singing, and soon for playing music, and my eagerness to spend hours by myself practicing. Later, as I became a serious organist and then, later still, when realized about my sexuality, I would come to see my organ playing as a sure sign of my sexual orientation; for almost every male organist I knew turned out to be gay. Perhaps it was also in the joy I felt at church, in my sensitivity to spiritual things, my delight in the music there, in the love and acceptance I felt there as a child, my sense that I belonged there—a sense that seemed to be greater than that felt by my peers.

Puberty had hit at age twelve, and I shot up to a skinny strapping six feet. My peers started to notice the girls differently, and they started talking about the girls, but I started noticing guys. It was all very confusing. I had questions, but nowhere to find answers.

Now Peter, age sixteen and a camp counselor, was inviting me to move to a bed next to his. That night, he seduced me. I was a very willing participant, and it was a wonderful experience, for we talked a lot and many questions were answered. I was pleased at last to discover that there was a whole category of people who felt as I did, and I learned what they were called; I heard the word "homosexual" for the first time. I realized I was not the only one in the world with these attractions, and I also had some enjoyable lessons on what "we" could do together to express our attractions. Indeed, so much did we enjoy what we did that we continued doing it throughout the youth camp—discreetly, after lights were out. It all seemed very natural; there was no guilt at all–yet.

Peter grew up and married, became a pastor and worked for the church, and eventually become a union president in Australia. He later would offend me greatly, given our history, by writing to the presidents of Avondale College and the conferences in his union before my research visit to Australia and New Zealand in 1986 telling them to be careful of me because I was a "gay activist."

I was still very naïve on the subject but determined to do something about it. I guess I showed my academic bent, for I first turned to the library. For several months, when I was fifteen, I traveled with Dad to Brisbane, the state capital, every month. While he attended a conference committee meeting on those Sundays, I went to the big public library and looked up everything I could find on homosexuality. There was not much available in 1955. There were mostly accounts by shrinks of men who had come to them with "homosexual problems," often called, as I remember, "inversion." It was pretty depressing, but I read some of them several times; I felt a kinship with those men. I am not sure what my parents thought I was doing in the library. Certainly they did not know my actual interest!

In my last couple of years in high school, I had a friendship that unexpectedly developed into a sexual relationship. I would say that it was experimental rather than romantic. We did a lot of bushwalking together, and somehow often ended up naked in the grass. He, too, married later.

Guilt came about the time I went to college. I was still pretty naïve and isolated. There was not yet any gay movement, of course, especially in Australia. There were not yet any gay bars, even in Brisbane—not that I would have gone to one! However, after I moved to Brisbane to go to the university, I gradually discovered that "my kind" met in certain parks and other indoor locations known as "beats," and I gradually spent more and more time "cruising" there.

My sex drive was really strong, and I realized it was easy to find sex with men, so I became quite promiscuous. I longed for the romance I saw between my straight friends at church, but there seemed to be nothing there for me. I was strongly attracted to a friend there, but I could not even let him know.

All I could find was quick sex acts with strangers. I felt so bad after each that I would pretend I did not know the guy if I saw him again. Since I rejected myself, there was no possibility of forming a relationship with anyone. I was intensely lonely. I prayed all the time for God to take this away, to change me; I cried, fasted. I knew instinctively that I could not tell my parents, nor go to anyone in the church for help. They would only condemn, and I did that already to myself.

I had become personally much more involved in church, and now, for the first time, I started to feel guilty about my feelings and behavior. I cannot put my finger on where that guilt came from; I guess it was all around me in society. It may have also come from the fact that I was dating women because that was expected, and they seemed to be attracted to me. I realized I saw them as friends, not romantic objects, that there was no sexual attraction at all. Sex before marriage was not expected in Adventist circles, especially from a fellow so active in church. Although I could hide behind my "high morals," I felt great confusion and guilt.

Through these years, I never had a gay friend. Once I had sex with a guy, he knew my shame, so I was totally embarrassed should I see him again. I remember forming close bonds with straight friends and then feeling intense loneliness as they developed romantic relationships with girls. Because no one knew my secret, and this included my family, no one knew the real me.

Eventually, the tension became so great that I yearned to "change." I knew instinctively that I should not talk with a pastor about my "problem", so instead I went to the head of the counseling service at the university. This was early in my time in grad school. I don't think he was judgmental. His main comment expressed amazement that I was doing so well academically while finding the time to do all that cruising. Since I wanted to change, he offered me the best tool available to psychologists then—aversion therapy. This involved showing me slides of "dirty pictures," and giving me a small electric shock when the picture was a naked man but allowing me to "enjoy" a naked woman photo without interruption.

This did not make me straight! Indeed, it caused so much turmoil that I cruised much more frequently during that time. My reaction was to become even more promiscuous. I tortured myself, wondering if it might be Jesus' will for me to cut off my genitals. I became totally desperate–WHY DID GOD NOT ANSWER MY PRAYERS? My religious training led me to reject the method of "treatment." I felt I should be able to "choose" the right path rather than have my psyche manipulated into it. After six turbulent weeks, I broke an appointment and did not return, and then I realized what a relief this was. I was not yet admitting to myself that I was gay. This was something that I did, not what I was.

As my work in grad school progressed, I realized more and more acutely that I was romantically attached to my best friend who was, of course, straight. He, his girlfriend, and I often did things together. Weirdly, she always sat in the back seat of my car (Greg did not have one), and the three of us spent a great deal of time together both on campus and at church. There were many mixed feelings here–joy, frustration, jealousy.

Eventually, after we both graduated, Greg and I spent a year traveling overland, as much as possible, from Australia through Asia, the Middle East, and Eastern Europe to Scandinavia, where I received word that I had a post-doc at Columbia University in New York City, and had to leave him abruptly to meet the deadline. I remember sitting outside on the ferry from Lund to Copenhagen, crying my eyes out.

This was 1971. The gay movement was new and overwhelming initially to me. It was too sudden. In New York City, I initially repeated my Australian pattern: dating girls and having sex with strange men. I still did not think of myself as gay. This was not what I was, only something I kept doing and then repenting of and fruitlessly promising God I would never do it again. The remarkable thing was that I remained sure of my connection to God.

The struggle continued until I was 34. I was still deeply spiritual, heavily involved in church. Eventually, I thought through the significance of God's failure to answer my prayers. Surely God had the power to change me if He wanted to! Then maybe He did not want to?

In 1974, I helped a friend at church, a student living in the dorm at Columbia University, by putting up a visiting former classmate of his in my apartment. Even though Dick talked a lot about his girlfriend at Stanford, there was so much electricity between us that he looped back to New York on his Eastern tour; and when I returned home, there he was awaiting me in my bed!

Dick and I discovered we were mutually attracted to one another. This was something new; it developed into love. This made such a difference! He was not an Adventist, but of course I took him to church; I wanted to share all the important things in my life with him. Instinctively, I knew that this was good, that God was leading. Indeed, I found that in loving another for the first time that I gained important new insights into the love of God. Truly, it was "not good for man to be alone." I was in love, sure at last that I was gay, and so proud of everything that I told my church group at Columbia University about it in a sermon some weeks later.

The commuter relationship with Dick did not last, but I was finally out of the closet. Neither of us had had any experience in relationships, and we were unreasonably possessive and jealous, for having finally found love, it was so important to us. We had missed out on all the experiences most heterosexuals have as teenagers.

Along the way, I had dated lots of women friends. I was responding to social pressure and also to my loneliness. I was comfortable with these friends and enjoyed sharing concerts and picnics with them. The problem was that they often came to be attracted to me. I was considered good looking, intelligent, well educated, and I had become socially comfortable. They saw my failure to apply sexual pressure to them as compatible with my heavy church involvement. I am so glad that I did not fall into the trap of "turning on the romance" and marrying one of them, as so many gay Adventists have done. Indeed, those who went for counseling were often advised to "pray about it, date a woman, and marry her–God would make sure it would work out!" That would have been a recipe for disaster for both of us and for any children who might have resulted.

The next year I got mad about some academic put-downs of the new gay researchers at the convention of the American Sociological Association, put up notices calling a meeting of the "Sociologists Gay Caucus" in my hotel room, which overflowed, and I was elected the first president. A year later, I argued with the incoming president of ASA after the business meeting, demanding that a session on homosexuality be included in the program the following year. After five minutes, I was told that the conversation was coming out all over the ballroom through the speakers! That was how I came out in my profession, and that was another step. There are now several sessions devoted to us each year at the ASA meeting.

My chair at Hunter College, where I was teaching, was a conservative man whom I liked but whom I felt I could not trust with my news of being a gay activist in the profession. When he retired and was replaced by a black radical, I decided it was now time to complete the coming out process at work. But the new chair turned out to be a closet case who was threatened by my openness, and he then made sure that I would not be re-appointed for the next year. I was not yet tenured, so on a yearly contract. But it all worked out after some months of acute anxiety.

I found a new job, with a promotion to Associate Professor, at Queens College–and what could be more appropriate for me? At Queens College, I later discovered that the chair who hired me was gay, so my orientation disappeared as an issue. I feel so comfortable that I regularly come out to my classes at their first meeting. I remember how important it could have been for me to have a role model when I was in college.

In 1980, I was heavily involved in arranging the speakers at the first Kinship Kampmeeting. I guess that was my coming out to the denominational leaders, because it required scary phone calls to people I had not yet met inviting them to speak, a meeting with a General Conference Vice President, and finally phone calls to Neal Wilson, the General Conference President then.

Finally, after I felt increasingly good about what I was doing in Kinship, I was at last able to come out to my parents. If I had told them about it early in my life, it would probably have been in the context of "I have this problem," and I would only have brought them grief because they would not have known what to do. I felt it was great that I could do it in terms of "I have been doing some really exciting stuff in the church, where I am sure God is leading, and I want to tell you all about it." They took a while to digest that mouthful.

I could also tell them I had four gay cousins. We had grown up in different countries and in three different denominations, but this was clearly a family trait. Just as I had taken a long time to accept myself, I could not expect my parents to embrace the news immediately. They had to have room to ask questions, to mull over the answers. I had to be patient when Dad wondered aloud what was "wrong" with our (extended) family. I found that for a while the traditional roles were reversed. I had to be there for my parents rather than they for me, at least in this matter.

For me, coming out was a long process. A couple of years ago, my nephew came out to me. He is very glad to have a gay uncle.

I have been with my present partner, Scott Wager, for more than a decade. We are officially "domestic partners" registered with the local authorities, and we have a strong sense that God has led us. Indeed, looking back, I realize He was trying to lead me for years when I would not allow myself to follow. I was much more attuned to the prejudice around me than to the leading of God.

While many of my gay Adventist friends seem to have encountered only rejection at church, and have often left in despair, my experience has been different. It has been a mix, of course, but I have received a lot of love and support. I am very grateful to God for that, and to those who have been so supportive.

I have been very fortunate to be the Adventist chaplain at Columbia University for almost 25 years. They are a loving, searching congregation that thrives in its diversity. Scott is active there, too, as the organist. When they learned that we had become formal domestic partners, they got together and planned a great formal party for us as their celebration!

They were delighted with the story of how, when we came away from signing the papers, which occurred at the college where I teach, Scott exclaimed, "We just got married!" He grabbed my hand, and we then walked that way down the long corridor in the very building where I teach my classes.

Those giving support ultimately included my parents, whose love for me led them to accept me. In 1989, I took Scott home with me for the first time. When they saw us together, they realized how much we meant to one another. After a few days, Dad got us all together, told Scott how much he and Mum liked him, and formally welcomed him into the family. There were tears all around that day. It was one of the best moments of my life.

Ronald Lawson was born in Australia in 1940 to a family heavily involved in the Adventist Church. He completed a Ph.D. in history and sociology in 1970, and moved to New York City in 1971, where he was a Professor at the City University of New York and the Adventist chaplain at Columbia University at the time of this writing. Sadly, his partner Scott Wager has since passed away.

I Am Gay, Seriously

By Mervin Magee

I sure hope that the church will one day change its views about gay people. I don't think they can effectively help bring gay people to Christ unless they take a fresh approach to the situation. I think there needs to be an open dialog with a lot of prayer and Bible study to make a difference. Eventually, I think the church will slowly change from the inside out. I know that when church members find out they have close friends and family who are gay, then they are usually more sympathetic and understanding to the situation.

I've been trying to think of ways that might help the church change its views. I thought that there needs to be a wave of gay people coming out of the closet, so that the church can see there are many gay people amongst them that are wonderful Christians. I understand some people can't be out; but if those that can, will come out, I think it will help those who do not have gay role models in the church. If out gay Christians are strong and have a bulletproof faith, then they will help make a difference in the progression of the Advent Movement. Only with the help of the Holy Spirit and faith in Christ will people's hearts change towards gay folk. I hope things change soon.

In my coming out, I've had wonderful support and acceptance from my family and friends. I'm very thankful for them and their support. Otherwise, the girls at church are all wanting to go shopping with me now. I found it amusing that many of my friends have always wanted a gay friend. So, yeah, my coming-out experience differs greatly from the conventional way of coming out. I came out over the internet on *YouTube*. It's been a very positive experience.

Mervin Magee is a young gay man who came out on YouTube.

Kinship Kalendar

By Juliana Harvard

"Here's info from the latest issue of *Dimensions*," Teri wrote in e-mail. My online lesbian friend had typed a long list of gay community organizations and phone numbers for Dallas/Fort Worth, along with brief remarks. I perused the list. At the bottom there was a single word—Kinship—with a Dallas phone number and Teri's remark, "I have no idea what this is <shrug>."

My heart skipped a beat—I knew *exactly* what Kinship was! For several years, I had been receiving a monthly newsletter from Pastor Jan Marcussen, an independent Adventist minister in Illinois, whose focus was on the Second Coming of Christ. He had even published a well-known book, *National Sunday Law*, which was being distributed by conservative SDA congregations.

I had seen videos of Pastor Marcussen's sermons, and was thoroughly enchanted by his sweet, soft-spoken homilies. Only one thing spoiled the picture—his vicious homophobia. He described in detail the horrors of Hiroshima, specifically how those who were unfortunate enough to be in direct sight of the infamous atomic bomb were not only blinded instantly, but felt their eyeballs melt out of their sockets. He then declared that *that* was what would happen to all the unrepentant homosexuals when Jesus comes. Somehow, even in my deeply closeted state, that concept had very questionable credibility.

But one issue of Jan Marcussen's newsletter had stood out prominently. The front page displayed a bold headline about a "gay Adventist church" that was being sued by the denomination for using its name in *their* name, "Seventh-day Adventist Kinship, International." Jan Marcussen's purpose in the article was, of course, to point out the high level of corruption that existed in the mainstream church and in society. That the lawsuit was *not* won by the church totally eluded me as I took a deep breath. *There are more church members out there who are like me! Where are they?*

For many years, I kept this snippet of knowledge in the back of my mind. *Just in case I ever have a reason to find these people.* Now, in the spring of 1993, I was still married to my second husband and living with him and our two teenage children. But in the late night hours at my computer, I had I found an entire gay/lesbian community in cyberspace, through *America Online* and *Prodigy*. During my inevitable "coming out," I found other lesbian wives and mothers, like me; and I found other gay Christians.

During that time, I reached a totally satisfactory resolution of my struggle to reconcile my sexuality with my spirituality. I found a whole denomination of open and affirming congregations, the Metropolitan Community Church, and located a local one in east Fort Worth. Through a series of *ah-ha* events, I became completely convinced that it was okay with God that I am gay. But I had found no gay SDAs. I had looked for Kinship in the yellow pages at the same time that I had looked for a local MCC [Metropolitan Community Church], but had found nothing. Now, before my very eyes, in an unwitting e-mail from a tough dyke in San Antonio, was a real Kinship telephone number in Dallas! So, on a quiet Sabbath afternoon in April, when my husband was at work, I dialed the number with shaky, sweaty hands.

"Hello," began the pleasant male voice recording on the other end of the line, "if you are calling about the house for sale on Glenview Terrace, please leave your name and number and we'll get back to you." Beep. Silence. Click.

I dialed again, more unsure than ever if I really wanted to do this. I listened again to the message, then said, "Hello? I, uh, was trying to reach someone about Kinship—I hope this is the right number. I live in Fort Worth, but I'm a married woman and I can't give you a number to call me back. So, er, um, I'll try to call again...sometime." Panic. Click.

In my next moment of wondering what to do, I absentmindedly flipped through the first e-mails that I had received from my online SDA friend, Pastor Ron, and found something I had totally missed the first time. The sentence that began, "We do have several gay members–open as well as closeted," continued with, "and one in our area is a leader in the Kinship group. I have written articles for their magazine, and also serve on a special 1-800 crisis number for gays that operates through Andrews University." I would later learn about

Kinship's monthly newsletter, *Connection*, and the toll-free 1-800-4GAY-SDA hotline that existed at that time.

Hurriedly, I sent another e-mail to Ron. "Do you ever see that Kinship member who goes to your church?" I wrote excitedly. "Would you be able to find out if there are Kinship members in Dallas?"

Ron wrote back almost immediately with, "Yes, Rosemary and I see Larry often. The Kinship contact in Dallas is Floyd Poenitz and his number is (214) 707-1971." Same number! Once again, this time with full confidence, I dialed. And, this time, the pleasant male voice answered live.

"Is this the right number for Kinship?" I began.

"Yes, it is," Floyd responded, and I could hear the cordial smile in his voice. "Are you the woman who has left a couple of messages in the past week?"

I blushed. "Well, probably, but there was this recording about a house for sale."

Floyd laughed good-naturedly. "Oh, that! Yes, Lloyd and I just bought a new house, but the old one is still on the market. What can I tell you about Kinship?"

I began by explaining about my marriage, my children, and my frantic spiritual dilemmas. "I do want to know more about Kinship and other gay Adventists, but there's just no way I can have anyone call me or have anything mailed to me."

"I understand," Floyd said. "I was married for several years, too. My ex-wife and I are still very good friends. Occasionally, Lloyd and I have dinner with her and her boyfriend."

"Really?" I was astonished. "And do you go to church in Dallas?"

"Usually Central Church," he answered nonchalantly, "but sometimes we drive out to Grand Prairie or Arlington. Once in a while, we even visit Keene."

This is truly amazing! This man sounds like he could be a minister, or at the very least a good church elder. Can he really be gay? For the next two hours, I poured out my heart and soul to Floyd Poenitz, who listened patiently, understandingly, and spoke with kindness and lots of common sense.

"We have monthly Kinship meetings," he told me, "usually at my house. Wish you could come sometime, but I do understand if you can't."

I wished with all my being that I could sneak off to Dallas on a Saturday evening, but I knew I didn't dare. Still… "Are there very many women in your Kinship group?" I asked, trying to sound casual.

"Hmm, well," Floyd stalled, "not very many. There was one lesbian couple from Keene who used to attend. Haven't seen them for a while. In fact, I'm not sure they're still together." *Lesbian Adventists living in Keene?!?* This was almost too much to believe.

I sighed, almost trembling. "Oh, Floyd, thank you so much for taking time to talk to me today. You don't know what a godsend you are!"

"No problem," he smiled back. "I'm always glad to help a sister or brother. Call any time you need or want to. I'll keep you in my prayers."

I kept Floyd's phone number tucked away in the back of my wallet. Perhaps, someday, I would call him again. That "someday" came sooner than I had imagined. Within the next three months, I went through the emotional trauma of losing my "straight" best girlfriend who refused to admit to her sexuality after I came out to her. I spent a frustrating weekend with a single lesbian I met online and who visited from out-of-state then got "cold feet." I shared a fantasy week with another lesbian mom from another state and fell in love with her. Then I "lost" my firstborn son to a self-supporting Adventist boarding academy after having spent eleven years homeschooling him.

By the end of the summer, my husband had threatened divorce, suicide, and homicide. Life for me became extremely turbulent. My counselor later described it as "going through a wind tunnel." I called Floyd to "cry on his shoulder," even though I had never met him in person. I spent another wonderfully peaceful Sabbath afternoon on the phone with this understanding, compassionate, and thoroughly loving Christlike man.

Then he called me. "Kinship is having a pool party at my house on Labor Day," he said. "I know you might not be able to come, but I wanted to let you know about it." Then, "Oh, yes, there *is* a woman in Keene who told me it's okay for me to give you her phone number. Her name is Janelle Radclyffe."

By this time, my husband had ended up in a mental hospital. When he was released after a week, he was given restraining orders to stay away from the house, though I didn't know for how long. So I called Janelle—the very first gay Seventh-day Adventist I was to meet in person. I invited her over for Sabbath dinner, and she accepted. When I answered the door that bright August day, I was stunned. She looked so normal!

After a meal of Special K® loaf and green bean casserole, we spent a lovely Sabbath afternoon together. We discovered we had both attended the same Adventist college, but we had never met during the one year our college attendance overlapped. We discussed our mutual passions for writing and teaching and John Denver's music. We laughed a lot. By sundown, we had gone from being total strangers to feeling like we had been very best friends all our lives.

The very next week, Janelle took me to the Labor Day pool party at Floyd's house. I met David Morris, a former academy teacher and fellow organist. There was Jodie and Tom and Kevin and other Kinship members in Region 5. Later there was my computer buddy Charlene who I worked with at Microsoft. I could share anything with her, from the spoofy country-western song, "I Spent My Last Ten Dollars on Birth Control and Beer, (Life was so much simpler when I was sober and queer)," to deeply serious Bible studies as she pursued her own spiritual journey.

Occasionally, we'd meet Kinship members who were visiting from out of town. There was Walt Elias, who would later become a *Connection* editor. There was beloved Adventist pastor Mark Edwards who was in the middle of coming to terms with his orientation, and another extremely talented but most necessarily closeted Adventist musician affiliated with a major denominational institution. And, always, I continued to marvel at how "real" and "normal" gay persons are!

Janelle and I attended Kinship meetings together regularly. Month after month, we met on Sabbath evenings, usually at Floyd's house, for potluck suppers—a most delightful experience when gay men are turned loose in a kitchen! Floyd always had a business meeting to discuss future Kinship plans. Somehow, Floyd even talked me into "doing" the regional newsletter, which we called "Kinship Kalendar," for a short time.

Many times we had animated discussions in Floyd's family room as we devoured vegeburgers or spaghetti, freely sharing an assortment of topics, from unabashed humor to the "anti-gay" Bible texts. Sometimes we went to other places, like Putt-Putt or Botanical Gardens or the Black-Eyed Pea restaurant. Other times we watched videos or went swimming. And often we ended up at The Roundup, a country western dance bar in Dallas' famed gay district, Oaklawn—the Castro of the Midwest. It was there that Floyd—despite being the smooth two-stepper that he is—was a most patient and uncomplaining dance instructor for those of us with two left feet.

Perhaps the best times of all were the Sabbath school and church services at Floyd's house, with David playing his keyboard, and with meaningful study/discussions, which affirmed that E. G. White admonition to "teach the youth to be thinkers and not mere reflectors of other men's thought."

In the course of my coming out over the next year, as I gradually "lost" my good Adventist friends and family members, my new Kinship friends became my family—brothers, sisters, nieces, nephews. Janelle and I fell in love, and she became the closest sister and friend I had always wanted but never knew existed. Through a horrendously ugly divorce that seemed would never have an end, Janelle and Floyd and the others provided a strong support system. Through my desperate quest for The Dream Job—or *any* job—my Kinship family was there for me. And loved me, no matter what. Whether I needed help to move a four-bedroom house or calming down from worrying about my rebellious 15-year-old daughter, I could count on my Kinship friends.

I no longer live in Texas. My life is in California, in the San Francisco Bay Area. But Janelle and Floyd are still only an e-mail or phone call away. The men and women in our northern California Kinship chapter have become special to me over these past months. And I even attended my first Kinship Kampmeeting in 1997. But perhaps nothing ever has had or will have the intensity of impact on my life or so perfectly fill my emotional, spiritual, and social needs, as did Kinship of Dallas in 1993.

Juliana Harvard writes about finding other gay Seventh-day Adventists through SDA Kinship International, Dallas Chapter.

Kitelover

By Leslie Quinn

I remember the first crush I ever had on another female was when I was three years old. She and her sisters were family friends and members of the Adventist church we attended. She and her sisters often came to visit us and I loved being with her, having her there nearby. I thought about her all the time and wanted her to love me special. I remember pretending she was my mother and spent hours making up pretend stories in which she would be my mom and I could always be with her. I pretended she would rescue me. That my parents were in constant turmoil and their marriage was a sham may have contributed to my need to be rescued. Mostly, I just wanted to be held and cuddled by her. To this day I remember her and the comfort that crush on her brought me during one of the terrible periods of my life.

As I grew older, I continued to have crushes on various older girls and women in the church or from school, and sometimes a teacher. I had long blonde hair and the older girls loved to play with my hair. I loved to have them play with my hair, too! In fact, I loved to be held or cuddled by these teenage girls. I liked to sit on their laps, which our small Christian school bus often accommodated. I would feign falling asleep in their arms so I could listen to their conversations and smell their perfumy scents. Sometimes I would slip their scarves or a hanky from their pockets and take it home with me overnight in order to extend the essence of my time with them. I would inhale the sweet scent and go to sleep, pretending to be held in their arms, my own arms clasped firmly around my pillow.

Occasionally, I developed a crush on a girl my age, but this usually ended up uncomfortably when I would try to give gifts or flowers to her. It was easier just to have crushes on the older girls or women, as they accepted the gifts I gave them much more gracefully and with a big, comfortable hug.

Then I discovered TV celebrities and had crushes on them. The various female stars I fell for were incorporated into my pretend world, and I made up stories with one or all of the women I cared about. Sometimes I would make up entire families, in which I was the youngest sister, with four or six big sisters. Sometimes I had only one big sister. And sometimes I would pretend that one young woman was my mother. The stories I made up became long epics, and then I had to write them out in order to keep them organized.

During these years, my father and a foster brother had molested me. I am sure my pretend world kept me sane and from splitting into several personalities. In my pretend world, I was rescued from the hurts and pain. I even could divorce my "father" from the family in one of my continuing sagas. It wasn't until years later, that I actually did divorce myself from my father for real.

When I was in academy, I still wrote stories about women I had crushes on. I tried to have crushes on the boys; but, you know how crushes are–they can't be forced. I had a couple of dates with one guy, but he was painfully shy; and I was very uncomfortable and would have rather gone on the dates with my girlfriends. It was very awkward to be all dressed up fancy. I developed a rash, as well as knocking over the golden-candled centerpiece at the table where we sat. It was awful, with hot wax running over the linen tablecloth and all!

When I was in college, I fell in love with the woman across the hall from me. She was engaged to be married, and I knew it was hopeless; but I still wanted her. My college years were upsetting and emotionally draining. I was constantly confused by my feelings and felt guilty and depressed all the time. I dated a couple of guys, but it always felt so unnatural and wrong to me. I hated when guys looked at me with desire, or with that lurid look. It felt so dirty. Even when a man would look at me in admiration, I hated it. That all felt so wrong to me.

Yet, my religion and church were telling me that homosexuality was wrong. I was in constant turmoil. I wanted so badly to marry and have a family. I wanted to be normal. But I think somehow I must have sensed that I wasn't "normal." I agreed with myself that if I *ever* found out I was lesbian, I would kill myself. So began many more years of denial. And many more years of crushes on women.

After graduating from nursing school, I fell in love with a woman nine years my senior. This one was different. This one reciprocated my love. We told ourselves we were just sisters and family, because we could not admit we were having a lesbian affair. The problem was, she was married, with kids, and a husband who often cheated on her. She made the first physical advances on me and I followed right along. It was the first time I felt loved and adored in my whole life, the first time I had ever felt beautiful, the first time I felt cherished. I will always be thankful for those feelings. But it was an unhealthy situation, not because it was a lesbian affair, but because she was married.

I finally moved away and began my life in another part of the U.S., still having crushes on other women, still denying I was a lesbian. I couldn't be a lesbian, because how would it ever fit in with being Adventist? And how would I continue to live, if I was a lesbian, since I had vowed to kill myself?

When I finally started psychotherapy for past sexual abuse, I threw my entire self into it. It was draining and hard work and very depressing having to deal with past abuses. But what a relief now that I look back. I had so much anger inside myself, and it had been spilling out all over my entire life. The therapist I had was a gift from God. I was finally able, with her help and acceptance, to talk about the abuses for the very first time. The anger finally resolved itself, and I began the healing process. However, underneath it all was still the lesbianism.

In therapy, I learned to be true to myself. I had surrounded myself with genuine friends who were very supportive. One friend, an Adventist physician, encouraged me to find out what I could about God and what He had to say about homosexuality, and especially what He had to say to *me* about it. That's when I began to know and love God authentically. She gave me the book *Servants or Friends? Another Look at God,* by Graham Maxwell. I also listened to his taped Sabbath School classes and began my journey, finding out how *very much* I was loved by God, no matter what. When I learned how different God was from what I had always thought Him to be, I fell in love with God, too! I learned God made us all different and loved the various ways we expressed our love and worshipped Him. I began to see God in a different light. In fact, I began relating to the female part of God. She became Amah God to me from then on!

This close connection I felt with Amah, and the love and acceptance I felt from God, allowed me to look at my life truthfully and not run away to kill myself when I realized I was a lesbian. And when I developed a crush on an openly gay woman at work, I realized I could no longer deny who I was. But before therapy and before finding out who God really was, I could never have addressed this issue in my life in a healthful way. The lesbian woman at work was the one who told me about SDA Kinship International. For me, it was the most wonderful thing to find out there were others just like me out there! God had brought me to this place!

However, I still had a way to go and much studying to do, until I could finally allow myself to be both Christian and lesbian *and* know it was okay with my God. But that is where I am right now. I *know* in my heart and am convinced that I am accepted and loved by God. I now believe in the hope of salvation that Jesus promised each one of us.

Before my mother passed away, we used to talk about what we each believed about God's stand on homosexuality, or rather, what she knew the Adventist stand on homosexuality to be, while I would tell her what I knew in my heart God's stand to be. She would quote me things from the *Review*, like "It is okay to be a homosexual, but not live the lifestyle of one." I had a lot of trouble with this, because if God made us to be sexual people and God made me a lesbian, why would any God *do* that to someone? Make her a lesbian, but say she can't ever have the love or expression of that love in this life? No God I knew would *ever do* something like that to someone S/he claimed to love.

For me, the word of God needed to make sense; and it had to reveal what God's character was like. I could not believe in something just because a church or religion believes it. That would be too much like being a servant. *My* God wanted me to be a friend, and wanted me to understand things clearly, not just do something because S/he arbitrarily said so! The Adventist church did *not* make sense to me in their beliefs about homosexuality, because I could *not* see this God in my life doing such a thing to me! And who in their right mind *wanted* to be gay or lesbian in the first place? How could it be a choice, as the church wanted everyone to believe? Who would ever *choose* to live as an outcast, a scorned member of society, church, and family?

My mom didn't have the answers to give me; she was too much a servant of God and of the Adventist church. And I could not go that route now that I knew God differently. We never settled anything between us about homosexuality before she died, but I know she loved me dearly, and I loved her as well. I look forward to talking with her in Heaven someday, having her meet the partner I met after her death, and sitting at Jesus' feet while He explains all these mysteries to us once and for all time!

I met my partner on KinNet, much to my surprise! We just seemed to click in writing and we had a lot of things in common. Before we met in person, she was the one who introduced me to the music of Marsha Stevens, the lesbian who sings gospel music for lesbians and gays. But the most memorable time for me was when my new friend wanted me to "listen" to Marsha's music with her over the internet. We were 2,000 miles apart, but she would adjust her CD to the same song my tape was playing so that we were experiencing those wonderful words and music of God's love together over the internet! It was a very spiritual thing for us, and I was blessed that night by falling in love with my partner and re-falling in love with God. What a validating effect on me to hear a Christian lesbian sing about her love for God! It was the music that validated me as a person who God loved no matter what or who I am! And it gave me rainbows of promise to continue on, no longer in the shadows of guilt or confusion, but walking in God's light!

Leslie Quinn is a pseudonym.

La Señorita de Tejas

By Sadie Roa

I was born into the Seventh-day Adventist Church (a conservative, yet very political and hypocritical, Spanish Adventist church), and have been raised in it all my life. I am currently an active member.

As long as I can remember, I know that I have been attracted to girls. I was a tomboy (still am), and one of those kids who used to dream of marrying Barbie, not Ken. I didn't understand why I felt that way about girls and started to think there was something wrong with my brain and me because I had been taught in elementary school that "boys like girls." I already thought I had some sort of mental disorder. Due to ridicule from the very feminine girls at school, I went from being very outspoken, loud, and flirtatious with my girlfriends, to being very shy and quiet. I was scared.

Then, in fifth grade, I finally learned what "gay" was. Still, I didn't associate or label myself as "gay," not only because I was in denial, but also because I feared what might happen if someone (church, family members, or friends) found out. Finally, in sixth grade, I came *out* to myself. I remember crying myself to sleep that night—happy because I'd finally found myself, scared of what was to come in the future, and sad because I felt I was damned to hell.

It was that belief that "homosexuals will burn in hell and have no hope for salvation," that horrible message of hate that I learned in the Adventist church, that nearly killed me. Before I had come out to myself, I felt very close to God. He was my Buddy, my Father, and I was a "Jesus freak," a very happy Christian. Then after I finally came out, I felt all that change. I felt as though I was now hiding from God. That, as a homosexual, just waking up was a sin for me because my "lifestyle" was a sin.

Slowly, I slipped into depression. From the age of 14-16, I began to self-destruct. I felt, and still feel, that life is just not worth living if you're not working towards going to heaven. Therefore, I would mutilate my body; not severely, but just poke myself with a needle in order to focus on physical pain rather than my excruciating emotional anguish. I began to smoke and drink and experiment with drugs, such as pills like THC. I even went to where I overdosed on pills, not once, but twice. My parents just thought I was going through one of those rebellious teenage phases. They've never been involved in my life nor my school life, though I've had no problems in school. They also have never hugged me nor told me they love me. I've grown up mostly alone, without their affection and support.

During this period, I began to date. So not only was I going through personal and emotional problems trying to deal with my sexuality, but I was also dealing with homophobia in public and at school. My peers were, mostly, very supportive and accepting; it was some teachers who harassed my current girlfriend and me. We were constantly threatened and falsely accused of engaging in "inappropriate behavior." All of this stress got to me many times; thus, I attempted to kill myself time after time.

Then, when I was 15, the mother of a friend of mine found a note from her daughter to me talking about me being gay. She freaked out. She not only beat her daughter but also called up all of her friends, our mutual friends, and talked to their parents about what a sick person I am because of my sexuality. She said that, because of my sexual orientation, I was a threat to their children. She said I abused drugs, though I had quit by this time. She said I was a pervert, the leader of the gay group at school, and a bad, very bad, diabolical type of influence.

Some parents bought what she said some didn't. Mine did. For she called my parents and told them all of that and more. And, since my parents had never been involved in my life, they believed all she said about gays and who I am. That night, they yelled and yelled. They threw away everything in my room—all of my material possessions, electronics, my magazines that I do, my poetry, my books, any literature I had, my homework, schoolwork, everything but my clothes. They said I hadn't been born that way, and therefore some outside influence had taken over and was now controlling me.

My father (who physically abused my older half-sister her whole life and has mentally and emotionally abused my mother throughout their whole marriage) threatened me a lot. He kept telling me I wasn't, and am not, normal; that "my condition" had probably come from my mother's side of the family. He told me

I was to never mention to anyone that I had *had* this little problem. Also, my parents told me I better "turn straight" or they would take me out of school and put me in a Christian anti-gay boarding school. After I was outed, one of my male gay friends was thrown into one of those by his parents who discovered he was gay. Of course, I was scared, and I told my parents that I would go straight. Ugh! It still sickens me to think about that.

Many of my friends were very supportive during this time. One teacher even offered to take me into her home since my parents were so very willing to throw me away. And things continued to be horrible for me until...

Until one day, as I was sitting in a school bus with a Christian friend of mine, he told me that instead of believing all this garbage about gays and hell, to research about it in the Bible myself; to ask God directly for the answers; to look for support in him—and I did.

That saved my life, and today is my inspiration and motivation to live on to help other GLBT Christian youth understand the truth. Since then, I have developed a very close relationship with my buddy Jesus. As with all Christians, it is a struggle to do what is right and stay "on the right path," but that's a struggle I'm never willing to give up on.

On a different note.... I felt I couldn't end this story without mentioning another event that changed my life. Soon after all this chaos had died down a bit, I met my first love, Blanca. We went out for a year and 8 months. She broke up with me this summer after she discovered she has some sort of chemical imbalance, resulting in manic-depression mental problems. Some things she has just recently come to terms with. She changed my life a lot and gave me two of the best years of my entire life. I still love her, now as a friend, and continue to be her friend. Currently, she has been engaging in self-destructive behavior, so I've been under some stress trying to care for her and be her friend and all. But I'm learning to walk away and live my own life as well.

In conclusion, despite everything I've been through, I'm proud of who I have become, and am glad of where I'm going.

Thanks for reading my story. It's websites like *SDA WomynFriends* that could have saved me from developing the ulcers I got from the pills I abused and saved me from almost dying twice had I come across it at a younger age.

Sadie Roa was a student who wrote from south Texas.

My Road from Despair to Hope

By Ed Vieira

Going back as far as I can to my childhood years, I remember being five and being afraid of getting into rough play with boys, such as soccer games and all the other stuff normal for boys. My parents were in the bakery business down in Brazil for as long as I can remember; therefore, they were always too busy to dedicate very much time and attention to my two sisters and me. I felt lonely and did not have any friends. It felt like a vacuum inside. My two older brothers were ten and eleven years older than me and had moved away to live with our older sister who had just married. They would have nothing to do with my parents' new faith. The Sabbath thing did not sit well with them. My parents had accepted Adventism when I was three and had become very strict with my brothers. They had converted from the Congregational Church. Initially, we belonged to a split group called "SDA Reform Movement," but later on the family left that group and were accepted by the Adventist church.

At age seven, I had my first crush on a boy during second grade in grammar school. Then I fell in love with one of my friends in church at about the age of ten. I was never really in love with any women growing up. During the teen years, all my friends were talking about girls, but in my mind it was always a mystery trying to understand and see things as they saw them.

By the time I was a teenager, my attraction to men was very strong, and I dreamed about what an older guy would look like naked. From the very beginning, I was attracted to masculine-looking men, preferably well-built, muscular, hairy men. We lived conservatively and had a very religious Adventist upbringing, and all of those thoughts and feelings made me feel very guilty and ashamed of myself.

Not having a neighborhood high school in Brazil, I had to take a commuter train to travel to my school near downtown Rio every day. Being about fifteen then, my gay feelings were burgeoning, and I always checked out the men in the train and on the way to school. One guy in his mid-thirties would always find his way to be close to me on that packed train trip, almost daily; and as soon as he got near me, he would start fondling me in different ways. I felt uncomfortable yet enjoyed it somehow.

After high school, and at eighteen, I attended a newly opened Reformed Church school, three hundred miles away from Rio, in Sao Paulo, the largest city in Brazil. I felt that if I could get to know more of the Adventist message and be involved more closely with it, God would help me overcome this strong, so-called "perverted" sexual drive. It was not long after making that decision that I found out things would not change.

While at the school, I was much closer to other young guys my age; and it was easy to see they were having their own problems dealing with their sexuality. I could almost identify the ones who, like me, could also be gay and confused and not know how to act. Even though this Reformed Church was a very strict sect, while we were living in rooms that were more like barracks, I realized some guys were being sexually active.

I grew up very shy and could not open up to anyone. Being there away from my family increased my awareness of my sexuality. Once in a while, some of us would go to a sauna run by the church; and that presented me with a chance, for the first time, to be naked with other men in a private environment. These were guys were a little older than me, and at the sauna there was a lot of teasing going on among them. The church, being very strict, would not allow intimacy between guys and girls; and the guys tried to follow closely whatever Ellen G. White had to say about that. One could see those guys had a lot of sexual frustration inside.

At the school one Sunday morning, a very prominent minister came up and asked every one of the male students if anyone in the school staff had offered any of us sexual favors. I immediately knew who the person was he was looking for. This custodian guy of about forty, and very friendly toward all the male students, had been getting into sexual relations with some guys, one of them a close friend of mine. I remember him trying to get very close to me, but something in me always made me refuse his advances.

As I got older, at about twenty-two, my gay feelings were so strong I started becoming nightmarish about finding a man to have sex with at least once. I was losing weight, had little appetite, and developed migraines. Then I got involved with church music, playing the organ and directing the local choir, to forget about that "monster" inside me.

A year later, I became part of the main Adventist church and was given a job at the Brazilian SDA publishing house as a printer, since that's what I learned in high school. After trying to date two girls, I met a third girl who was also very shy and reserved, having also belonged to the Reform Movement herself; and six months later we got married. The strangest thing is that during our dating we never kissed even once and were never intimate.

A week before my wedding day I became so desperate, I went to a cruising place in the city and tried to find a man to have sex with. An older guy of about thirty invited me over to his high-rise apartment, but after one hour of trying hard to do something together, I could not do it and left. My guilty feelings took over, and I felt incapacitated at that moment. In the elevator on the way down from his place, I looked at the people around me and felt they all knew what I had just done. (The Adventist Church can really teach us how to feel guilty about many things.)

The day of my wedding could well have been the day of my funeral. I felt trapped and unhappy like never before.

After four years working at the publishing house, playing the organ for the local church and directing the choir there, I had made a few friends singing in a quartet. One by one those friends were immigrating to the U.S. The last one to leave told me a few days before taking the trip, that if I desired, he would find a way of getting me to immigrate here. I told him that if he were really serious, I would take his offer of help. Sure enough, less than six months later, we were all gathered together as a quartet in New Bedford, Massachusetts, at the end of June 1965. Except for the bass of our former quartet (who later came also), we sang together that first Sabbath in Worcester, Massachusetts, using Doctor Puyanna as the bass. The doctor had sponsored me as an immigrant just because of his love for quartet music.

Three months later, our former quartet bass arrived. He lived with us in our large three-bedroom apartment. This was a handsome Brazilian guy of Italian-Portuguese background. I had been in love with his looks and personality for the last four years, and now having him under the same roof was an unbearable situation for me. He was also a friend of the other guys who had immigrated before us. Our friends called on weekends, inviting him to go to a park to play basketball and to be part of other activities. Since I had never been sports-minded, this started to cause a conflict among us. I developed jealousy toward them because of their invitations to him and I could not hide those feelings very well. Soon my wife started to notice it. I always felt my friend could be also gay, since at twenty-eight, he was not dating girls but hung out with a lot of men all the time. At that point, my life had become a daily nightmare, and I didn't know what to do. I thought I would just go crazy.

In the middle of all that turmoil, being under a lot of stress and having lost my friend's confidence, one night I noticed he did not come home until late at night. I could not sleep thinking about him. At about 2:00 a.m. I went to his room to see if he was there. Sure enough, he was in bed but not asleep, with open eyes just as if wondering. As I approached his bed, he grabbed my legs and pulled me closer and grabbed my crotch area. That caught me by surprise even though I felt it to be an opening to talk about our feelings. But as I started talking, telling him how much I loved him, he stopped me dead by reminding me I was a married man. I left his room and went back to lie by my wife.

The next morning, Sunday, my friend left for work very early since his boss had asked him to work that day. I was worried about what could happen next. I drove to his workplace to have a talk. By the time I got there he wasn't showing any interest in having a conversation with me, but I noticed by the reaction of some of his co-workers—some mutual friends of ours—that he had told them about what had happened the night before. I had never felt so scared and lonely in my entire life before that day. I went back home from that place crying all the way, asking God why he had allowed me to be born gay to suffer such embarrassing moments in my life. That same evening, my friend moved out of my house, and a few days later went to live in the D.C. area.

A month had gone by when the pastor of the local church called a meeting for all of us to clarify what had happened. Among our friends, stories of all kinds were being told of what had happened, most of them to our embarrassment. The truth was apparently not being told. My friend came up from D.C., and in the meeting there were a lot of denials and different versions of what had happened. It was also announced that my friend would marry one of our other friends' sister-in-law, a single woman who had had a crush on him from before. All this was being done by our group of friends to clear my friend's name, while letting my name go down. They did not want people to think he was gay, and he fell for their demands, marrying the girl later on. These supposed friends used the opportunity to get this guy to marry their sister. Had nothing happened I'm sure my friend would not have married under such pressure.

The trauma we got into was so heavy, three months later I moved my family to California. Then, fifteen years later, while I was living in Redlands, California, I received a call from that same friend asking me to forgive him for all the damage he had caused in my life. He said he had lied about us, and that he had lived a terrible life and needed to be forgiven. Also, in 1981, some of those mutual friends of ours came to visit us and we took them into our home and treated them well. And even though not a word was said about the past, we could tell they also wanted our forgiveness.

By 1975, I was taking some classes at a college in downtown L.A.; and when the classes dismissed early, I would stop in Hollywood to see what I could find out about gay life. It started to dawn on me I could not live in denial all my life. I still had not had sex with men during all those years.

Then my in-laws came to visit us from Brazil. My wife's sister's husband, Tony, a light-skinned Italian hunk thirty years old, asked me if I could take him to see Hollywood Blvd., while the girls went shopping in Glendale with the kids. Once there, looking at the stars on the walk, we stopped at a large newspaper stand that offered everything, including gay magazines. I noticed pictures of men and advertisements of bathhouses in them. My brother-in-law actually pointed them out to me, which made me wonder about him. To make the story short, I went back one day and looked up one of those places and went to see what it would be like. It was there I had my first encounter and knew that that was what I had needed all my life. I had finally come home. Sex with a man fulfilled all of my internal needs.

In 1984, after not having had any sex with my wife for six months, she confronted me one day, asking me if I was gay. At first I denied it; then, after a couple of hours of reflection and having realized that that was my opportunity to be truthful once and for all, I asked her for a conversation and told her the whole truth about my homosexuality.

The next day, my wife came home with an address and date for us to have an appointment with an Adventist therapist, a doctor in La Sierra, who would try to help me overcome my homosexuality. When we left his office, we came home with a list of things we were supposed to do as soon as we got home. It had to do with getting intimate with one another as we had never been before. The thought of it made me sick inside. If, during our twenty years of marriage that had not happened, how could it happen then? We had two kids during our marriage, but our sex had been very businesslike. There was never a genuine enjoyment of being together as it is with heterosexuals. Even before we got home from the doctor, I told my wife that I would try to do all those things, but that I was sure it would not work. Sure enough, after trying to follow the doctor's program for fifteen minutes, I got up and told my wife I could no longer force myself to do things that seemed so odd and abnormal in my state of mind. At the end of that month, we separated; and I went to live with my first roommate.

Days later, my daughter found out from her mom why we had separated. She wrote me a letter assuring me she would always love me as her dad no matter what. My daughter had many gay friends in high school and has always been open-minded about things. It took a few years for me to tell my son about my sexuality. When I told him he said he already knew it, and that his mom had told him about what made us get separated. Even though he's been good to me, as a devout Adventist, he thinks it's wrong to be homosexual.

One day after work I was visiting with my wife (we never ceased being friends), and she said to me she had had a conversation with a woman pastor at the University church in Loma Linda, and that she had told her about our situation. The woman pastor gave her a phone number of a Kinship organization and a local contact (Bernie Ochoa) I should call. The pastor had said to her that the organization could be what I needed and that they would probably help me and cure me from my deviation. (I don't know to this day where that pastor got such a misinformation.) I told my wife I was going to call the number, adding that something made me feel inside that these people would not try to cure me if anything was to happen. A few days later, I went to my first Kinship meeting in Glendale at the home of Dr. John Weiland. I took a gay friend along for backup, since I was very apprehensive about meeting a bunch of Adventist gays. When we arrived there and were parking the car, I saw a young man carrying what looked like a potluck dish, going in the direction of the house (Jeff Lombardo, my first crush in Kinship). Then I thought in my mind, "Hmm, if the guys in Kinship look like this one I think I'm going to enjoy being here." My next reaction was... Wow! Gay Adventists like me, and they do not intend to change me at all! It was heaven on earth!

The next day I told my wife about my visit with Kinship. When I told her what I learned while there, she could not hide her disappointment. My wife really loved me, and I just wished I had been heterosexual to return such sincere love coming from a wonderful lady. I've always believed in my heart that if I had been heterosexual, I would have had one of the most wonderful wives in the world. My ex-wife was neat, responsible, smart, and a perfect mother. She was also very good-looking, being of European heritage. Her Hungarian grandparents had come to Brazil in the early 1900s.

Now I was free to be myself. Yet something was missing. I became very promiscuous for the next four years, frequenting bathhouses with friends for sex, trying to get as much sex as I had always wanted through the years. For a while, that was what I did on weekends. One day in the middle of one of those places, I was so tired of all the cruising and afraid of catching AIDS. I stood in a corner there, and in a fervent prayer to God I asked Him if He could pick among all those beautiful men there present, one to send him my way, one I could keep. I even asked in my prayer that this person need not to be someone that lived in the gay community, since I had had unpleasant experiences with guys from the community. I was tired of all of what I saw happening in the clubs, and I wanted to stop going to the baths.

It was not even a half an hour before this well-tanned man with an athletic body stopped next to me and invited me to follow him. After our first encounter, I asked him if he wanted to stay in touch. He said yes to that, and the rest is history. We have never missed a weekend away from each other since unless he or I had to go on a trip. We will commemorate our 14th-year anniversary this September 2, 2002.

Ed Vieira was born in Brazil at the end of 1939. At age 18, he left his home in Rio, Brazil, to attend college classes in Sao Paulo, the largest city in that country. At 25, by the invitation of friends, he immigrated to the U.S., where he became a citizen in 1980. Ed has worked as a classified employee for San Bernardino Community College District for the last 24 years. He has lived in Colton, California, near Loma Linda, with his partner Clark since 1988.

My World

By Mark Edwards

As a Seventh-day Adventist pastor and a married man, I struggled for years in a private hell from which there seemed no escape. As a minister I felt I had no one to turn to and, as far as I knew I was all alone in a frightening and traumatic dilemma.

But I'm getting ahead of myself. As a child, I was basically very happy during my growing-up years. I came from a loving, two-parent family and my parents were proud of me. I was considered a "good" Seventh-day Adventist kid growing up. My parents being missionaries, I had wonderful opportunities for getting the experience that only travel can bring. My father served in many church leadership positions, from mission director to division president—a legend in his day.

During my adolescence, no one talked much about gays–the word was not even in common usage then. I grew up in remote mission fields in a conservative family where sex itself was never discussed. In retrospect, I now realize I can hardly blame myself for being so late in discovering my sexual identity. I also understand how the mind can play strange tricks to deny the obvious, especially when acceptance is too painful or incongruous with one's belief system. I *knew* I couldn't be like those strange homosexuals with their outlandish behavior and costumes I occasionally read about in the media. That simply wasn't me. (It still isn't!)

So how old was I when I first understood who I was? I don't really know for sure. For me, it was a gradual, sickening awakening to the fact that I simply wasn't the same as others. I don't believe I knew who I was when I married. I was once again making "the right choices" in life. Despite my sense of humor, I have always taken life seriously. I had never engaged in premarital sex–straight or gay. I had high ideals for marriage (I still do) and wanted to make a happy home for my wife and children. The option of not marrying simply did not occur to me. Why even Paul himself said it was better to "marry than to burn," even though some of his ideas on marriage are hardly considered the norm.

And so I continued to deny the inevitable. My conservative church upbringing did not prepare me to accept the overwhelming sense of devastation and aloneness I faced when I finally admitted I had a mental attraction to men which no amount of praying or fasting would change. Yes, I believed God could do anything, but He chose not to answer my pleas.

I will never forget the day I finally came out to my wife Nancy. True to form, I had planned months ahead of time when I would tell her who I was. I would wait until a week after she had graduated from her course, so that the news would not affect her studies. I would then tell our teenagers a few days later.

It was without doubt the hardest thing I have ever done. I was literally sick to my stomach for months before the date I had chosen. I kept arguing with myself that there really was no reason to tell her anything. I even got melodramatic, telling myself I would die alone with the secret I held. I wasn't even "living the gay lifestyle." (I hate these euphemisms: does anyone "live the straight lifestyle"?!) But I also knew it was time to be honest. I was living a lie. While our married life was, to all outward appearances, normal, I knew the mental torment I was going through to conceal inner longings that Nancy could never meet.

I also knew that, at some level, Nancy knew that all was not well, and that I was hurting her. "I sense there's a barrier between us," she said on a couple of occasions. I just scoffed at her words, terrified that she might guess the truth. *I* knew what she meant, but I knew she didn't really understand.

So that Friday evening, with our teenagers away on a church campout, I finally told Nancy about the real me. Knowing my tendency to joke, she didn't believe me at first. When it finally hit home, we both sobbed on each other's shoulders for what seemed to be an eternity. For her, it was the beginning of a nightmare; for me, it was as if the weight of the world had been lifted off my back. To her credit, never once (then or since) has Nancy blamed me for being gay or tried to convince me I could change my orientation.

In my own planned way, I knew full well what the consequences could be. I knew our marriage would probably break up (this is something Nancy and I both eventually agreed on). I knew it would be difficult for our kids to accept; though they too have been amazingly understanding through it all–far more than I expected. I knew I would probably lose my pastoral career. Although the news of my story did not break for several months, when the conference finally found out, I was given no choice but immediate resignation with no severance pay, despite many years of service with a spotless record. Though I am pretty agreeable to most things, I felt this was unfair; so through negotiations with the conference, we reached a considerably happier settlement.

Do I regret my decision to come out and be honest? I regret the considerable pain I have caused both family and friends. I regret having lost my vocation as a pastor with a Church that I still love and support. But not for one moment am I sorry that I was honest about myself. I just wish I had decided earlier in our marriage—if I had been able. It would have been easier on Nancy, though perhaps not on the children.

To those who ask, "What makes a person gay?" I reply, "What makes a person straight?" No one knows, no one really understands. And what does it mean to be gay? Certainly, this is *not* all about sex, as some believe. We are talking about a whole different mindset in which a general sensitivity (often including strong proclivities to music and the arts) makes itself clear. Clichè, perhaps, but still true.

In the meantime I hope the Adventist Church will no longer take an ostrich-in-the-sand approach but face the reality that its gay brothers and sisters are everywhere in the Church: from congregational laity to college faculty, church pastors and General Conference workers. We are hurting and isolated, and as much in need of denominational acceptance and the forgiving grace of Christ as anyone else. Please don't continue to ignore us.

Mark Edwards is a pseudonym.

Partners in Parenting

By Emily Thompson

Ever since I can remember I have had a close relationship with God. When I was about ten or eleven years old, my mother read a few entries in my diary that suggested homosexual activity. She came to the doorway of my bedroom as I was falling asleep and in a nearly hysterical voice, demanded me to stop my behavior, stating it was an abomination to God, and threatened that I would go to hell if I didn't change my ways. From that point on, I prayed to God for new feelings, to change my attraction from Barbara Streisand to Robert Redford. I put up posters of David Cassidy, Bobby Sherman, and Donny Osmond, among others. I had trouble falling asleep at night and experienced vomit-inducing migraine headaches until I was baptized into the Seventh-day Adventist Church at twenty-two.

Although my mother had been raised Adventist, I was not. She left the Adventist Church when she met and married my father. I was first introduced to the Adventist faith when I began to spend time with my Adventist aunt and uncle and family. Because I had maintained a personal relationship to God and Jesus throughout my childhood, when I was near graduating from a public college, I started going to the small Adventist church that had at one time been the home church of my grandmother. Before traveling overseas to student teach in Wales, I was baptized and accepted into that Adventist Church. My traveling companion was my Bible, and I spent many hours reading and meditating about the God who created and loved me. I will never forget the feeling of newness that enveloped me as I rose from the baptismal waters. It wasn't until I arrived at my host home in Wales that I began to realize what Jesus wanted to teach me now that I had turned over my life to Him.

When Dora, the woman who greeted me, took my hand to welcome me into their home in Wales, I felt a strange and warm sensation. Even though I had been active in sports and was surely in the company of lesbians during my college years, I never discussed the topic with anyone or even with myself. After a few weeks of living with my host family, and witnessing to them about my faith, Maggie, a 40-year-old mother, confided in me she thought she was in love with her best friend of over twenty years. I had to travel across the ocean to a small town in North Wales to meet my first lesbian. She unwittingly opened the floodgates of feelings that I had been almost successful in burying deep within me, seemingly out of reach. I read my Bible and prayed with new fervor.

My first teaching position after returning from Wales was midyear, in a tiny town in rural Nevada. When I was introduced to Jane, the teacher whose classroom I would take over, she shook my hand; and once again, I felt that same strange and warm sensation. This time I thought, "She is a lesbian." Several months later, Jane confided in me she was indeed a lesbian. And several more months later, I realized I was in love with her; and my "great conflict" began. As I struggled to reconcile my true sexual orientation with my faith, I entered the most traumatic year of my life.

My mother confronted me again, this time about the true nature of my relationship with Jane, this female teacher. When I reluctantly acknowledged her suspicions, she grew hysterical and launched into an abusive pattern of preaching, name-calling, and rejection. My Adventist aunt reassured me they still loved me but opened their Bible to share the verses that she thought condemned me.

Then Jane, my first love, left me for someone else. Our principal asked us to resign our teaching positions because some anonymous person accused us of being homosexual and therefore immoral. As one person summed up: I had lost my job, my love, my family, and my church—what else was there to lose? Fortunately for me, and for anyone else who will accept His gift, I had my personal relationship with God and Jesus.

In addition, I found SDA Kinship, a support group for current and former Adventist gays, lesbians, bisexuals, and their families and friends. Through my association with Kinship and the Kampmeeting experiences, I found the acceptance and reconciliation I had always longed for. I came to believe that God created me and loves me for who I am. I now know that when I turned my life over to Jesus, it was the beginning of my journey of self-acceptance, and that Jesus led the way.

Today, I am a lesbian mother with two boys, Ryan, age four, and David, eight months. My partner Grace and I had been together for almost four years before we inseminated. However, we had already experienced parenting together as a couple.

Only a year after getting together we assumed the parenting responsibility of my sister's then five-year-old daughter because my sister had lost custody of her daughter Alexa to the state child welfare system. This child came to us with severe emotional problems (violent tantrums, biting, head banging, and other forms of self-mutilation), together with IQ scores that showed she was mildly mentally retarded. In the two years we parented my niece, she gained 16 IQ points, discontinued all of her self-destructive behaviors, and used complete sentences instead of two-word phrases. At age seven, Alexa was returned to my sister and her second husband. Today, she is living in a psychiatric residential facility for adolescents. This is her second placement since being returned to her heterosexual family.

The experience of raising my niece Alexa only magnified my long-standing desire and belief that I would be a good parent, but I thought my sexuality condemned me to being a really great aunt. Although lesbian couples were having babies long before me, I didn't consider it an alternative until I met my Grace, my life partner, in 1990. We had a Holy Union ceremony in 1991.

After reviewing the sperm bank alternatives, we asked a very close gay male friend (from SDA Kinship) who had been in a monogamous relationship for seven years if he would consider being our sperm donor. We proceeded only after Conrad submitted to and passed the same testing sperm banks used to screen donors. We contractually agreed that he would have no legal rights or obligations; and when Ryan was two, we had a judge end his legal rights. The same procedure will be followed with David.

As Grace and I expected, notwithstanding our contract and the donor's legal status, my four-year-old Ryan has discovered that he not only has two mommies, but he has two daddies as well. We have expanded our concept of family accordingly. In addition, our boys have three grandmothers, two grandfathers (one passed away), and plenty of aunts, uncles, and cousins to shower them with love. If only all children were so carefully planned, wanted, and loved.

Our family life has many more similarities than differences to a healthy heterosexual family life. We are preparing to move to a bigger home with either a guest house or room to build one because we know we will be the adult children who take care of our parents when they can no longer live independently. I truly believe that both Ryan and David will grow up to be good, decent people who will make the world a better place. They already have.

Emily Thompson is a pseudonym for a real-life Adventist lesbian mother who lives with her partner and their two children in mid-America.

Philippine Memories of a Gay Adventist Youth

By Pag Mamahal

Bakla, Bading, Bayot, Binabae—those were the names I was called when I was growing up in Manila. I wish the Filipino language had an affirmative label equivalent to "gay." Instead, I was teased with the hurtful words—*faggot, sissy.* Even before I entered elementary school, I remember my aunt telling me not to walk like a girl. I was always teased in Sabbath School because my buttocks would sway even when I was running, and my wrist was limp.

My second-grade teacher warned me not to hang out with girls too much. I don't know; I just couldn't play with the boys—they always called me names. I wasn't used to being treated like a weakling. I was always dominant at home and I wanted to be the leader.

The girls were the only ones who were nice to me in school. How I wished I could be like the other guys! I remember watching my cousin's Pathfinder group marching on the school grounds. I was attracted to their leader. One time I saw the leader and his friends playing basketball. They didn't have their shirts on. I kept staring at them and watched their bodies sweat.

When I was in sixth grade, we learned about the parts of the body. Most of the boys talked about how they would experiment with "things." They talked about how sexy girls were. They wished they could kiss and hug the girls they had crushes on. I didn't feel that way. I wanted the affection of a *guy*, not a girl. I couldn't resist my attraction to men.

Maybe I just wanted to be like the other boys. Maybe I just wanted the entire church school to stop calling me a sissy. To be a "bakla" is a sin, according to my mom. She told me when I was eleven years old to be careful with a "bakla." *He might even try to kill you.*

My father, who is an ordained minister, cautioned me, too. "I heard that your school director is a 'bakla,'" my dad warned me.

My best friend from elementary school recently mentioned to me that his parents forbade him to hang out with me when we were growing up because he might be "bakla."

So, how can I stop people from harassing me? *I can't be "bakla" if it is a sin.* But it's impossible for people to condemn me. Even my first childhood memories remind me I was always called "bakla." *I couldn't have been born with a curse.* It is like being born deaf, just like the character from the movie, *Mr. Holland's Opus.* But my church cares for *them*—the disabled, the alcoholic, the drug addict, and the divorced person.

I have been attracted to the same gender for almost twenty-five years now. I am not sexually addicted to the same sex. All I want is to be treated normally, like the straight people are treated. I cannot help not having feelings for women. I always fall in love with men. Do I have this feeling because I was labeled "bakla"? Would I be different if I had the courage to tell my parents that I was attracted to the security guard I kissed on the cheek when I was a baby? They knew I loved kissing and hugging, but they didn't know that I had "different" feelings with the boys or men I hugged.

I thought it might have been a lack of a father figure. My dad was busy preaching in different churches. But I remember my dad teaching me how to ride a bike, how to swim, how to skate, how to use a stick-shift car. He walked me to school. I even have his temper and his habit of finishing the leftover food.

Yes, we are all born sinners. But is my "sin" so bad that I would be condemned? Romans 1:27 doesn't talk about a guy *falling in love* with another guy. I don't care about the sex part. I know how it feels to be in love. You don't fall in love because someone has sexy legs. It is a feeling you can't explain.

I tried so hard to feel that with a woman. I know how to detect a beautiful woman. I had lots of girl "crushes." Or, at least, I told my friends that because I knew who the beautiful girls were. I was obsessed with a girl in high school. *Oh, she will be my partner in life.* But I just couldn't feel what my other guy friends were feeling.

It wasn't until I was nineteen I felt the magic of love. (I had come here to the States when I was seventeen to go to college). I became close to a guy, and I didn't know he was gay. We were so close that I wanted to be with him forever.

Then "it" happened. I thought guys just do "it." Hey, my guy classmates in the Philippines were talking about doing "it" together (I always wished I could join them!). Then he asked me, "Are you gay?" I couldn't answer.

I spent the entire summer reading books on homosexuality and men's studies. I studied about ex-gay ministries, what the Bible says about homosexuality, and about verbal harassment. I cried to God, "Why have you made me suffer all these years?" *I don't deserve to be discriminated against. I am happy and at peace with myself when I am with a man.*

I've learned that in Hebrew, there are different terms for homosexuality; and that the term in the Bible is for someone—a straight man—who lusts for sex, for doing "it" with another man just to fulfill his libido. I am not that way.

When I accepted myself, that I was born gay, I found my inner peace. I stopped suffering. But I continue to search for answers. I continue to seek His will. My parents tell me that they are concerned about my salvation. But I know God doesn't want me to live my whole life questioning myself. I don't want to end up feeling like I am always having a nervous breakdown because I was born with a "mental disorder." I know I am already saved by God's grace. Should I spend the rest of my life trying to cure the "sin" I felt when I was born, when I didn't even know anything about this world?

We all know that we shouldn't be judging one another. It is up to God. I hope and pray that I am not the only person experiencing since birth the feeling of condemnation from my church members. But many Filipinos have come out to me. It is by chance that we learned about each other. There is nobody to talk to because preachers are condemning gays. There isn't even a good word for the term "gay" in the Filipino dictionary. Maybe things would be different if gays were approached with love. Would we even know how to deal with it if a five-year-old boy approached us with a comment: "I think he's cute"?

There are those here in the United States who have brought up their children to accept the difference of a person. We may not give an answer to the five-year-old boy. But one should not assume that Jesus says homosexuality is wrong. I don't have an answer to why I've felt this way since I was born. All I know is that I still love my Lord, and that I am happy that He created me.

I am happy I'm gay, I'm happy I'm gay,
With Jesus Christ, I'm happy I'm gay.
He has taken all my sins away.

And that's why I'm happy I'm gay.

(sung to the tune of: "I'm Happy Today")

"Thank You, Lord, for creating me. I know you would treat me like anybody else. Just like when you were at the same table with Zacchaeus, and just like when Mary Magdalene poured oil on your feet. I know you want me to be happy with a partner, just like when you found someone for Adam. Am I meant to be alone on this earth because I was born not liking Eve? All I know, Lord, is that I have found happiness and peace through accepting myself and through the assurance of my place in heaven. My faith looks up to Thee. Amen."

Pag Mamahal is a pseudonym for a young gay Filipino man.

Search to Find

Anonymous

This past weekend I probably have slipped to the lowest ebb in my life, but I'm coming up. My life has been one unusual experience after another.

Ten years ago I was working for the denomination, was married to a wonderful lady (but not in love with her), and I was in love with Mike. Mike and I had two and a half years of wonderful life. Yes, there were difficulties that finally ended in my leaving the relationship, and I went back into my "perfect family situation." No one ever knew! It was a stormy breakup, but Mike and I loved each other even in the separation. He went to his mom, and I went into hiding my feelings in my church work.

I broke off complete contact three years ago. This past Sunday morning Mike's mom called me to let me know he committed suicide Friday night. Mike and I had this thing on keeping the Sabbath, candlelight dinner, a lot of hugging, reading to each other, music that gave us both a spiritual high together. I never knew it, but Mike got his mom into the same Friday night mode for the past seven years (Mike was not an Adventist). On Friday night, she was setting the table, and he put the music on and went into his bedroom and ended his life.

Mike's dad came down from The City and they had him cremated. Sunday morning they found a letter to me in his room with my current phone number and called! Mike and I had planned to live together forever and die together, so we bought this urn eight years ago for our ashes to be mixed together and sprinkled in the river. Mike's mom is keeping the urn and his ashes for me. He told his parents that I was the only one who loved him. I found out Sunday his big secret that tore us apart! He had been abused by his dad.

These last two days I think I have been in hell, if it weren't for two people on KinNet who have been lifesavers. You see, I joined KinNet about a month ago.

I still blame myself for Mike's death and can accept part of it, but after crying about five hours in the dark tonight my stereo came on in the lightning storm. This is the miracle—I never play the cassette, only my son when he was here three weeks ago—and my Father turned it on just when I needed it the most. Here are the words from the chorus of "Hope"—the only song on the cassette:

"Hope you in the Lord and renew your strength
Soar you up on eagles' wings
Tirelessly run the long race that's set before you
Your life's a song the Father sings.
"Hope that you can see is really no hope at all
And like children who see faces in the clouds
We hopefully listen to the silence of life
and find that it is shouting out loud.
"Though your life may seem to sound a dark and minor key
It will someday shift itself to major
And the lyric of your life will rhyme
With nothing less than joy,
And you'll know that hope is from
The One that you believe."

You see, my favorite song is "On Eagles' Wings"—only God knows that! But He played this for me. Now maybe I can sleep! Shalom.

Anonymous

Sharing a Journey

By Vickie Shelton

MEETING AND DISCOVERY

Although neither of us remember exactly when we met in the mid-60s as students at an Adventist college. We lived separately in the women's dormitory and had separate circles of friends. For the first year or two, we knew each other only in passing. In the spring of 1967, Emy Lou asked me to room with her during her senior year. I had a year plus a semester remaining. Knowing her to be a gentle, fun-loving person with a truly marvelous wit, and because I'd not made other plans, I agreed. It was a wise choice!

In the fall of 1967 (we cite August 26 as the date), we moved into overflow apartments where upper-class women were to live. It was a lovely setting with a living room, kitchen, bedroom (twin beds), and a bath. We studied and conducted our college business pretty much independently through the first semester. Christmas break took us separate ways—she went home, and I visited another friend at an Adventist academy nearby.

After returning from vacation, we realized how immensely glad we were to be together again. Probably right then, but no later than during the first several days of 1968, we knew our love and friendship was special; and it has remained so to us every day since. The intimacy we have been fortunate to share on all levels—emotional, physical, spiritual—during our lives together makes us profoundly grateful. It is a gift we covet for every one of our friends.

ACCEPTANCE/COMING OUT

From the beginning, we knew we'd have to reconcile church teachings with our lives and relationship. Celibacy was never a long-term option for us. We knew our lives together and our expression of love was a beautiful thing for us, but we also knew others might see it differently if we were to disclose the nature of our relationship. Because scriptural conflicts and religion were greater concerns for me, these issues troubled me more; but we each continued on some level to struggle with our sexuality as we moved to our present home state and each began our careers in "the Work."

A breakthrough came on the concerns which most troubled me when dear friend, Larry Hallock, with his understanding of Greek and scriptures prepared and shared his own coming-out story with his family. His essay of 1975 or 1976 was the first I'd read, which suggested interpretations for those texts other than the condemning interpretations I'd learned.

The rest, as they say, was downhill because at about that time books on the subject became common. During our college days, there was nothing on the subject in the college library other than a very old medical book, which described homosexuality as an illness. As books became readily available, I read everything I could find and became convinced our sexuality and loving expression of it within our committed relationship was perfectly right and moral for us.

In summary, our coming-out process began with personal acceptance, continued through sharing among close friends and acquaintances, then with family members—both families—who have been highly supportive, and ultimately generally to almost everyone in almost every situation. As I've often said (quoting Kinship writer, Bob Holland), "Although we don't always choose to disclose our orientation, we no longer fear its discovery."

THE STUFF OF LIVING

We consider our life to be very similar to anyone else's. We work, decorate, renovate, recreate, garden, volunteer, vacation, entertain, and parent puppies and kitties. In short, we live. We do the same things of living you do. We do the same things of living our neighbors do.

Career/Finance: Home ownership began for us in 1975. We believe this kind of intermingling of financial and day-to-day property responsibility is important to relationship permanency, particularly for same-sex couples. Because we have no other legal obligation to remain in relationship, a mutually shared financial responsibility can create an additional reason not to bail if things get tough. Since whatever problems we may have would likely be carried into another partnership, it has always seemed preferable to us to work through issues than to bail.

We each ultimately left denominational employment and feel much better for having done so. Presently, we have our own business and consider ourselves to be semi-retired while enjoying our work *and* needing to work to prepare for senior years!

Problems: Every relationship has them. Ours is no exception. Fortunately, we have worked through all concerns which have surfaced so far! Some issues have been significant, others better fit a "misunderstanding" category. In every circumstance of conflict, we are committed to talking things through carefully while remembering two guidelines: 1) we are permanently committed to each other and to our relationship; and 2) our bottom line is, we *love* each other. Parting ways is not an option, and so far neither of us has wanted to do that.

Sexuality: Yes, even women in their 50s (we are 55 and 54 at the time of this writing) enjoy those exquisite intimate expressions of love. If we ever lose the need/desire/capacity, we'll let you know. I've always been curious about this aspect of aging, so I suppose you may be, too. But don't expect to be hearing from us!

We wish for every one of you the depth of joy we've shared all these years.
Vickie Shelton is a pseudonym.

Sunshine

By Phillip

I knew I was gay before I married, but it was something I didn't accept as being part of me. I don't know whether it was caused by genetic factors, pre-natal or post-natal causes; I just know that I didn't deliberately choose to be gay.

I've been told I was a sweet, blue-eyed kid with blond curly hair. My Oma (grandmother) often called me her "Sunshine." All anyone could see was this kid with a ready smile for everyone. But something happened which caused me to withdraw into a sullen world where that bright, untarnished smile vanished into hurtful distrust. And the struggle is still continuing.

I remember a traumatic experience that happened when I was around three years old. My 21-year-old cousin was very fond of fussing over me and taking me around with her to different places. One day she set me on the kitchen table and disappeared into the bathroom. When she came back out, her breasts were exposed and her nipples were smeared with jam. I felt choked with fear. I burst into tears and screamed. Waving my arms about, I distracted her from forcing herself onto me. Sheer bolts of fear flashed through my head as I sobbed, wanting to go home. This isolated experience affected me so much that whenever I saw a baby being breastfed, I would shake with fear and would run out of the room. I've only recently been able to recognize that this was an episode of abuse. The bright, sunny smile I presented to the world gradually began to fade.

My dad, a tall handsome man with jet black hair and piercing blue eyes, thoroughly enjoyed outdoor life. Dressed in his old army greatcoat and slouch hat, he would often take his dogs and rifle and go hunting in the forest surrounding our home. Or he would drive to a nearby river, take the fishing rods out of the trunk and cast a few lines. Back then he was a wonderful dad, someone I looked up to. I enjoyed riding on his shoulder and feeling his unshaven face rubbing against mine. I would scream with laughter and playfully push him away. But something happened which seemed to put a distance between us.

Dad adored my mother, who was a loving, devoted wife and mother. Because of circumstances unknown to me, we shared the house with my grandparents and I guess that was a strain for her, since she is a fiercely independent woman. An excellent cook, she taught me how to cook. Often we would sit at the piano and I would try to imitate her playing. Later, I taught myself to read music and play the piano. My dad tried to get me interested in boys' toys, like match box cars, a tiny pedal car, ball games, and even taking walks with him in the dark, green forest. I enjoyed the walks but was very frightened when he raised his rifle and fired at some object or animal. I would hide in the shelter of his great army coat. Despite my dad's efforts, I was always more attracted to dolls, high-heel shoes, and smearing my face with my aunt's lipstick. Dad began to sense my indifference and occasionally mentioned to my mother that I was a sissy. This was something I couldn't understand.

As I grew older, I learned I was hearing-impaired, and the distance between dad and me increased. I was frequently told to say words properly with little help. Faced with a harsh world, I retreated into a world of books, dreams of a better life, and wanting to be loved and accepted. So I sensed very early that I was different.

Like many others, I was reared in an Adventist home where we had worship twice a day and attended church every Sabbath, often staying there until late in the afternoon. It was a very strict environment where the woman from Battle Creek and her books were constantly referred to. My early concept of God was clouded with fear and uncertainty. It seemed to me that He would pounce on me and punish me every time I did something wrong. I felt I had to be good in order to earn His good will. I had to be extra good to get to heaven. This later became a constant source of discouragement. Everything else in the world was "worldly". And "worldly" things—even people—were looked down on. Sex was definitely taboo. On two occasions, I was thrashed by my irate mother when she caught me "playing" with my brother's genitals. She belted me and said the police put people in jail for things like that. That stuck in my head, and I was riddled with guilt.

Part of my childhood was spent growing up on a dairy farm. Now and then we would drive 50 miles to the nearest big city and spend the day shopping. Once, when I was almost 12, I wandered down to the beach to wait for my parents. A lady clad in a brief bikini was lying on the sand, but I scarcely looked at her. I was captivated by the sight of the lifeguard. He was handsome and well-built, and just looking at him thrilled me.

No one warned me of the changes that would occur with my body; and as these changes became obvious, it caused me to be alarmed. I wondered if God was indeed punishing me. A friend of mine from church told me what was happening, and it was indeed a relief to discover that he was going through the same changes. I became attracted to him, and it was always a pleasure to be near him.

When I was fourteen, I was sent to a boarding academy in a neighboring state where I spent the next six years. There I found myself attracted to several guys. Feeling guilty, I tried to date girls; but there was nothing. Something wasn't right. Even when a well-thumbed copy of *Playboy* was passed around, I couldn't find anything there to arouse my curiosity. It disgusted me.

It was a very painful process to fully accept myself as a gay man. Throughout my life, I just knew that I was different; and when I heard the word "homosexual," although it came as a shock, it fully fit the feelings that I had. I was afraid of sports and so excused myself from them. One of my friends, remarking on some behavior which I found amusing, said only queers liked that kind of thing. I silently told myself, "I know I'm queer, but I can't help it." I just felt so isolated. Lonely. My self-esteem plunged to rock bottom.

After academy, I attended college for one year. It was very difficult for me to mingle in the communal showers they had there, so I got up very early to shower in order to avoid the company of others. I dated girls, but it was more like having a friend to talk to. If I was turned down, hot tears burned my eyes, because I felt they could sense that I was different.

I left college and went to work for the church-owned health food industry. Back then it was still taboo to even mention homosexuality. Doing so would have led to rejection, perhaps even the loss of my employment, and bring shame to my family. Being insecure and sensitive, I just couldn't talk about it—not to anyone in my family, not to my friends, and especially not to my pastor. It was something I could never look anyone in the eye and talk about; it was too shameful to mention.

I honestly believed that I was the only Adventist in the entire world who had homosexual feelings. Putting on a mask, I buried the secret deep down inside me. But I admired the courage of some people in the gay rights movements who appeared on TV. To cope with my internal stress, and perhaps to help me feel more manly, I took up smoking. This eventually caused me to be fired from my job.

Life was a struggle. I mingled with straight guys, did the same things that they did, tried to play football with them. I joked about gays, too, inwardly hating myself for doing so. My mother wrote to me, saying it was unnatural for me to be spending so much of my time with my friends.

Not knowing what to do, I began to think that maybe if I got married I would no longer have this gay orientation and be attracted to men. I came to firmly believe that this would solve my problem. While working for the health food industry, I had met a lovely young lady and decided that the answer to my dilemma was to marry her. Besides, I badly wanted to please my parents and feel good in front of my peers.

We married, and our wedding night was spent in a classy hotel sleeping on our own sides of the bed. Although there was various evidence that I was different, and I once accidentally left a gay newspaper in the house, I didn't talk to my wife about my struggles, because I honestly believed they would go away. Instead, my gay orientation grew stronger.

A year after we married my wife was pregnant, and I stumbled into a gay club, an activity which I continued from time to time. The gay rights movement became prominent, and I eventually left the church because there was no way I could reconcile my orientation with what the church taught. From time to time, I would earnestly plead with God. I just couldn't understand it all. I felt condemned and knew that the Bible said it was a sin. But I couldn't help it. It was natural for me to feel that way.

Finally, after eight years, and with two children in our family, I decided I had to tell my wife that I was gay. Inwardly, I was terrified about how she would react. So, I wrote out what I was going to say. Fear tingled up and down my spine as I watched her read my note. She responded by saying, "No matter what, I still love you." But not knowing how to handle this situation thrust into her hands, she made things difficult for me by "spilling the beans" to my parents, her family members, some church members, and several friends. This only caused me much heartache.

Being afraid to approach the church, and with no one offering me much-needed help and support, I plunged deeper into a pattern of compulsively addictive sexual behavior with anonymous gay men. Often after leaving such an encounter, I would sit in the corner of the sofa, bunch up my fists and groan from deep inside me, "God, please help me!"

I still firmly believed that I was the only Adventist to feel this way. But one day while browsing through a gay bookstore, I discovered a news item about a group of gay Adventists who had met together in the United States in a "Kampmeeting." A ray of hope dawned in my mind; but then I dismissed it, since it was far away from these shores.

The mid-1980s brought the dread news about AIDS and its impact on the gay community. It was a scary and stressful time. One night I had a dream which helped to bring me back to church and give my heart to the Lord. I could overcome smoking—just Him and me, working together. I still had the wrong concept of God and thought I had to be perfect in order to be saved. This was changing, but ever so slowly.

Prior to my being re-baptized, the pastor came to visit me at my home. I revealed to him my struggle, not only with smoking but also with homosexuality. I could sense his discomfort with the topic. He quickly told me he would never say a word about it to anyone. This only reinforced my belief that I had to overcome being gay.

I still wanted help. It had to come from somewhere. Earlier that year, my mother had sent a letter with a clipping attached to it, and I had kept it. It was a list of books and materials for marriages and relationships. But it was the last item, about changing from homosexuality to heterosexuality, that caught my attention. I found that highly amusing, but I kept the paper. Now I searched the phone book for the name at the bottom of the list and dialed the number. I asked about this list of books and where could I find the tapes listed at the end. I was told to contact the conference office and ask for the marriage counselor there. This was my introduction to Colin Cook's tapes and the Quest Learning Center.

I began counseling with a pastor, based on these tapes and other materials, and then with another pastor. For a while, this offered me hope I could really change and be "normal" as a heterosexual man. My hope of change was dashed, as time went on and I found my attractions were still as strong as ever. But the small ray of hope that I wasn't alone in this began to grow in my mind and helped me to fully accept myself as a person who was gay. I was still disheartened and discouraged over not being able to change. But my concept of God was changing, and that kept me hanging on because this became "news" to me.

I still had dark valleys to go through. Other times, the mountains loomed high and threatening above me. There were cliffs that were impossible to climb on my own. Sometimes there was nothing to hang on to, the nearest edge way above me or too far below. One pastor who counseled with me said that because of the fall of humankind, we are broken in all areas, including sexually. God sees us as very broken people who need healing. Because of that, he suggested maybe God is not too rigid with having monogamous relationships with another man. Healing and acceptance came to me slowly. Gradually I accepted myself as a gay man who is loved by God.

I tried, in some small way, to explain how wonderful God's love was to me as a gay man. When someone wrote negative comments about homosexuals in an Adventist publication, I wrote back that God's love was for all, including gay people. Since I had signed my name, there were some nail-biting moments as I waited for negative comments. There were none, but about six months later my mother wrote and said I had brought shame on the entire family by writing that letter. Although this lack of acceptance was shattering to my self-esteem and I became very discouraged, I continued to accept myself as I am, a gay man. This was very liberating, and for the first time in my life I began to feel like a normal human being.

I still had some hard lessons to learn, but I believe God was patiently drawing me closer to Him with each experience. During this time, I learned more about SDA Kinship Internanal, where I found acceptance and love that I couldn't find anywhere else. Although still living with my wife and children, I experienced love with another man. But the relationship fell through. I ended up going back to my lifestyle of clandestine sexual addiction, while maintaining my connections with the church. But each experience left me increasingly uncomfortable.

Then, several experiences caused me to change my thinking and focus on the Lord. First was a work-related accident. I injured my neck and later needed major surgery. Then there were long months of rehabilitation and efforts to get back into the workforce. Finally, there was a termination of my employment from an Adventist hospital, where I had so much loved working. In my despair, I went to gay clubs to escape my problems, but that only caused me to realize that there was more to life than this. So I turned to the Lord because, even though I knew He accepted me as I was, I just wasn't comfortable being addicted to anonymous sexual encounters with strangers. I turned it over to Him and said that it was His job to help me change this addictive behavior.

Although I still believe that a monogamous relationship with another man may be acceptable to the Lord, I have remained married. I am committed to my wife and children; and I am prepared to live a celibate life.

To the Lord's glory, I have been freed from the addictive sexual behavior for nearly two years now. Mind you, I still have hassles. It's easy to feel the pull of places and ponder giving into sexual addiction. But the Lord has started a good work in me and has not given me up yet. My salvation doesn't come from not going to gay clubs or being intimate with a close male friend. It doesn't come from being gay or straight. Nor does it come from falling on my knees and telling God all my needs and what pleases me or going to church and reading the Bible. My salvation comes from just accepting Jesus as my Savior and believing that His death and resurrection was for me. That's all we need to do to be saved.

Over the past couple of years, I have found little support in my church or among its members to meet the needs of gay men like myself. However, once I connected to the internet, I found better support, including KinNet, the "electronic chapter" of Kinship. I have made some wonderful friends. Some of my email friends have become like family to me.

My marriage has been hurt, and it has been very difficult. Presently, I have remained committed to my wife and children. The pain is still there; the scars remain. One of the fallen monuments that has to be rebuilt is one of trust. Never for a moment suggest that in order to change one's orientation, a gay person should marry. I firmly believed that I could change, but it was like telling a leopard to change his spots. Even during a painful marriage, the rainbow of hope still shines and it reminds me that healing does come from the Creator of us all. When everything appears to be impossible, God turns a hopeless situation into something beautiful for him.

My concept of God has changed. I view Him now as I first did with my father when I was a small child. He became someone who will greet me with a warm hug and I could hide in the fold of his robe when I feel a little threatened. He is a God of love, someone willing to bend down from His throne and to listen to my whispered cry for help.

My life as a gay man, even while married to my wife, has brought me closer to a loving God. And if He can accept me by being my friend and loving me, cannot the church do the same?

Phillip is a pseudonym for a gay man who writes from Australia.

Sweetness in Silence

By Misty Gardner

It began as a simple friendship. When I met Rose at the Deaf Club in one summer, she was on the verge of separating from her husband. She had four small children. Although I had never been married, and certainly was not a mother, I felt an empathy with her. I understood what it was like to be "used" by a man. I had known abuses that I never wanted to think about again, much less talk about. Plus, Rose was hard of hearing, and I am deaf.

I was born and raised as a Catholic and went to a Catholic Residential School for the Deaf. I had never really understood the Catholicism, just that I had to do what I was told and was taught to live with it. I had lost interest in the Catholic Church in my very early twenties. By then a friend invited me to a Protestant church, and I had realized that something there seemed more right to me than the Catholic Church.

I remembered how I had always been a tomboy. I had always felt an attraction to women, but I certainly denied being lesbian. In fact, even when I was in my early twenties, I did not yet know the realities of being lesbian.

During that time, I had a lot of affairs with men, many of which lasted only two hours. Once I was raped in a way that I never knew could exist and I was angry at it having happened, but I felt ashamed and stupid for allowing myself to be a victim. I had indulged in a lot of fantasies about women, but I would never have dreamed of coming out to another woman in real life.

After my mother's death, I abstained from all sex with men for a year until one last time shortly before I met Rose. She had kicked her husband out. Just a few days later, she approached me and seduced me. I was scared to death, but I wanted more than anything else to have this affair with her. Of course, I did not refuse, and it all felt so good. I was going through some intense emotional feelings because of the one-year anniversary of my mother's death.

Rose and I lived together in New England when I quit my job and went to Gallaudet University. I did not expect that Rose would go with me, but she did. Rose and I and her four children moved to the Washington area. Two months after the move, my father passed away on the day just before our fourth anniversary.

The following Thanksgiving, I was hospitalized for an asthma attack. Our relationship had gradually begun to fall apart, but we stayed with each other for two more years. To salvage the relationship, as well to deal with the many additional stresses in my life since moving to attend Gallaudet, I went for counseling.

Again, in April of that following semester, I had another serious asthma attack. My doctor had already warned me three times during the preceding week, that I should not wait so long before coming in to the E.R. for needed treatment. During that attack, I had a very frightening vision that seriously affected my thinking about my own life. While the E.R. staff was saving my life, I saw two angels, a black one and a white one, fighting nastily with each other to take my life. When I woke up from unconsciousness, I was glad that I was alive; because I was not ready for whatever the black angel would have taken me to.

I thought about that vision, which stayed with me daily, whenever I would have problems with Rose. Is it the relationship? Is it the schooling? Why was the white angel so kind enough to let me live?!

Rose was falling in love with another woman. She cheated on me. After the breakup, I tried going to MCC (Metropolitan Community Church) for a year, hoping to figure out what that vision meant to me. I thought about it and decided that my lesbian life was wrong, and that it was time for me to get out gradually. That vision was still hanging around, and I was trying so hard to figure out why it was still in my mind. I was still wondering what the black and white angels might symbolize.

When I got a new job at the local phone company, I developed a new interest and fell for Lula. Lula was not gay; she was a Baptist. I was still honestly searching for understanding about God, because of that vision that was still really bothering me. And so I became a Baptist. But I was not satisfied with everything I learned from the Baptist church. I was never comfortable with all that talk of going to hell. However, I stopped my "gay lifestyle," shunning it completely.

Around four years later, I became interested in vegetarianism because of my asthma problem. In February, I received a flyer invitation from the Silver Spring SDA deaf group to attend a four-session vegetarian cooking class. Well, I "knew" that Adventism was just a cult thing, from what I had been told, but I figured I would just ignore the church beliefs and go for the vegetarian classes.

At the first class I was shocked to see Penny, an old classmate of mine from Gallaudet. She faintly remembered that I was "gay" back then when we used to hang around gays. She was not gay, but she hung around with them because she was involved with drugs. I was never involved with drugs, but I enjoyed being with Penny. Now she was the wife of Roger Mitchell, the new deaf pastor-in-training.

During the vegetarian classes, I became interested in finding out more about the Seventh-day Adventist Church. Immediately I accepted an invitation to attend the *Revelation Seminar*, and I learned so much more about the Bible than I had while I was a Baptist. It took me eight months of trying to figure out what was right, comparing the Baptist church and the Adventist church; and I prayed a lot about it. Eventually, I became convinced about the Sabbath and the state of the dead; it made so much sense to me. I knew Adventism was right. So, by November, I was baptized and became a Seventh-day Adventist. Roger and Penny were the only ones who knew that I had lived as a lesbian before.

One time during the ensuing years, I was reading through the *Adventist Review* and saw an article about SDA Kinship. I was really shocked, but I denied myself the right to think about it. More than a decade passed.

About ten years later, during a time of depression I was going through, out of the clear blue I emailed an old lesbian friend I had known in Massachusetts. We had not talked for years. I found Bobbie Jo's email address in a note that someone else had forwarded me, so I tried it. She was happy to be in contact with me again, and I with her.

Then Bobbie Jo asked me, "Are you really happy now?" I did not reply to her question, but it made me do a lot of thinking about myself—and I had to admit that I was not happy.

One day in October, I was pacing around all day and praying over all my repressed emotional feelings. I confessed to myself: *I still love women. I cannot reject that.* I could get that much out to myself. Still, I was too frightened to really come out. Again and again, I prayed and did a lot of soul searching about my true inner identity. Only then did I realize I was actually hurting my identity by hiding my true feelings. After I finally completely admitted my lesbianism to myself, I felt inner peace at last.

I continued to explore the internet looking for Christian gay/lesbian groups, and eventually I found SDA Kinship International. At last! Here was someone—lots of them—who were Adventist gays and lesbians. I wanted so badly to talk with and listen to them online. Before I officially joined KinNet, a type of *listserv*, I was a "lurker" for about two weeks. Then I realized I truly had wasted all my years of not being true to myself, and it was a joy to know that there are Adventist lesbians and gays out there. Eventually, I decided to actually join and become part of the group. It took me a month to come out to them. When I did, this was the greatest joy I had had in a very long time.

Millie Strong was the first one who responded to me the very next day after I joined KinNet, and she soon became a wonderful friend to me. We emailed a lot for three weeks before I got up enough courage to meet her in person, though she lived in my local vicinity. The following weekend, she took me to the local Kinship Christmas potluck. From that point on, I felt very comfortable about myself as a lesbian.

I now understand what my scary vision back in the E.R. was all about. The wondering is all over now. As I look back on it, I realize it was about God's love for me. God gave me the privilege to live again so that I could look up and know that the Lord is there for me, and for all of us, with the true meaning of love. I truly believe that vision was part of what led me to the Adventist church and back to my true identity. I fully accept myself now as truly lesbian even though I have been so alone. This is my last church! Even though I visited several other GLBT churches, I will always "keep the faith" that I believe is correct. I also know that God loves me just as I am.

Misty Gardner is a pseudonym.

Teaching about same-sex marriage to children

By Jaime Townsley

I *love* how the video [referring to the "Yes on Prop 8" right-wing propaganda] says that teaching about same-sex marriage confuses children. Not to put too fine a point on it, but if teaching same-sex marriage confuses your child, then just how dumb is your kid? Of course, the truth is, it doesn't confuse children at all.

I'm not out to my kids yet, but I am preparing for it. One book I have is called *The Family Book* by Todd Parr. Each page talks about a different kind of family. Between pages such as, "Some families adopt children" and "Some families are big," one page says, "Some families have two moms or two dads."

My kids have read this book several times without really even noticing that page. But last week, my eight-year-old was reading it out loud to her little sister and brother. When she read that page, she paused and said, "How can families have two moms or two dads?"

I said, "Well, two dads or two moms could adopt a baby, or maybe one mom or dad already has kids before they meet the other person."

She said, "But two moms and two dads can't marry each other."

Thankful to be a Canadian, I replied, "Of course they can!"

Her response? Simply, "Oh. I didn't know that," and then she went on reading.

It didn't disturb her. It didn't confuse her. It just took a simple explanation that two men or two women could fall in love with each other. It was like when she found out broccoli tastes good with cheese—it was just a piece of information that she didn't know before but knows now.

—Jaime Townsley [deceased 2011]

The Loneliest Man on Earth

By Trevor Lewis

It was the summer of 1997, and a splendid summer it was. I had been attending a prominent Adventist college, basking in learning, polishing my professional skills and status. I never expected to fall in love.

I met Steve just two weeks before the end of the academic session. From the onset, I knew he was a wonderful Christian man. But I didn't know it was possible to fall so totally and completely in love. I felt very much like the country song, "Never been caught talkin' to the man in the moon."

I'm an "innocent" in many ways. I had been married to Marsha for 22 years, and never slept with another woman in all that time. I wish I could say the same about all the men in my life!

Now I realized I had never been in love in my life. I love Marsha but have not been "in love" with her. Nor had I ever been in love with any of the men. This realization caused me to confront the gay issue, and for the first time I felt good about being gay. I started to take my Christianity with me, even when I went into the bars. *Shame on me!*

I had trusted no one so much as I trusted Steve. I let down all the walls of my heart, and he did, too. We were not two souls, but one soul. Five hundred miles apart.

One day I could stand it no longer. I packed my clothes and left Marsha to be with Steve. I had done nothing like this before! We began a life together, only to be confronted with a "wonderful" thing called conscience, both Steve's and mine. He could not live with the thought that he was breaking up my marriage. I would not let him violate his conscience. *How do you separate two souls? Anguish... despair... even of life....*

The only promise Steve and I ever made to each other was that we would, at all costs, do nothing that would prevent us from making heaven our home.

We wanted an eternity of being together, doing the "Huck Finn/Tom Sawyer" thing in heaven, visiting all those planets, and making love in a very real heavenly sense. Forever. This was something we just could not sacrifice. And violating conscience was one thing that would do just that.

I went back to Marsha. She is a wonderful woman. She knows. My kids are in college now. I am broken-hearted. I am the loneliest man on earth. I am drenched in tears.

God has closed the doors to Steve and me, at least for now. *Can I trust my Savior? I hope I can.* Life on earth remains to be lived out. An empty shell kind of life is not much fun, but I see myself healing.

Trevor Lewis is a pseudonym.

The Woman of My Dreams

by Pearl Pangkey
    I thank the Maker of the stars for His amazing grace.
    It seems that I've looked high and low but could not see her face.
    The face of one who'd cherish me in happy times or sad,
    One who accepts my many faults and often says, "Be glad..."
    "Be glad for all that life has brought to make your life complete:
    Family, friends, good health and food, and for this chance to meet."
    I'd never thought I'd meet someone who'd love me just for me.
    Someone who'd look into my eyes and see what I can't see.
    I've found the woman of my dreams, the one I've waited for.
    She's everything my heart desires, all that and even more.
    She loves, accepts and honors me. She's someone I adore.
    We made an oath that we'll be together forever more.
    This woman who I've learned to love is staring back at me
    From the mirror in my bedroom wall, she's letting me be free.
    I'm free to think, to choose and feel as only I can do.
    For I'm the woman of my dreams, and that I swear is true!
    Pearl Pangkey is a poet, photographer, and athlete

Will you be my tangerine?

By Rainbow Bright

Call me a drama-queen or a hopeless romantic—I won't mind because I embrace myself for who I am. But acceptance of oneself hasn't been that easy for me, especially when the acidic reality of me being a lesbian has given me so many heartburns.

I can't say with much conviction that I knew about my attraction to women from early childhood because it was quite the opposite. Yes, I'd been a tomboy—I loved to wear shorts, play rough games...but I had "boyfriends." My childhood best friend can attest to the fact that not only did I have tons of boy-crushes but also, I was even the aggressor (would write love-letters). I prided myself that I could get whoever I wanted. Of course, the thrill of making a guy like me wore off.

In high-school, I still had my top 5 guy crushes, but due to circumstance and a drastic change from being home schooled I became extremely introverted. From then on until my first year in college, I was certain that I was straight (not knowing there was anything else but that). Besides, all I knew about gay people—which was mainly men—was that they act like women and that they're prevalent as beauticians and that my brother was teased since he's effeminate. Being gay was because people talked and walked a certain way. In short, being gay spelled disdain, derision, and great disappointment. It was just unacceptable. I knew I didn't want my younger brother to be gay or even be teased like my elder brother, and so I made it a point to play basketball, marbles, and karate with him.

So, I was just going through college like all the rest. Trying to figure out my purpose in life... and having been brought up with the fear of the Lord, my values were clear to me—family and friends were very important...

THEN love came unexpectedly...thus started the story of my first love. My Sunkist. We had such an ideal friendship. There was genuine concern, and we simply enjoyed being together. We loved each other. But when homosexuality lurked around us we weren't able to cope with the painful reality. She flung herself at the guy who's been courting her since high school.

It took me years to love again. But why did I have to fall in love with a woman again this second time around? Oh, but I didn't have to worry that much because she was already with someone. This time I held on to friendship, at whatever cost. Looking back, I knew everything was wrong from the start. Her track record spelled infidelity. She fell in and out of love too easily. Ah, but she was my *ponkan*. Very sweet...

If my first love was more of an intellectual attraction, then this time it was very emotional. So, the next that I ventured into was someone I'd been physically attracted to. My "dalanghita." She could be sweet, but she gave me a sour ending. She knew how much I loved my *ponkan*, despite all the heartache.

That's the story of my "love for three oranges" that I brought here to America. Wasn't that a very colorful life? I don't even like the color orange. That was my mistake. Had I known I'd like her...I guess I knew I was bound to like her but I knew she wasn't my type. I thought I told her soon...but it wasn't soon enough. My tangerine?

Rainbow Bright is a young Filipino woman, college student, scholar, and independent thinker.

Afterword: Gay Pride

By Floyd Poenitz

Gay Pride.... I think that many folks have a problem with that term for two reasons. First, the word PRIDE is something that many were cautioned against by parents and educators during the years growing up. Somehow, the terms Pride and Proud were two separate concepts. BEING proud was a positive thing. HAVING pride was "almost sinful." Sort of the Pride Goes Before the Fall syndrome. So the term gay PRIDE is difficult to imagine for many.

Second, so many gay Christians are still buying into the theology that gay is SINFUL or at least SECOND BEST to what God ordained and planned. With that line of thinking that being gay is not quite good enough, or at least inferior to being straight (the "goal" or ideal), then how can anyone really BE PROUD or HAVE PRIDE in themselves and what they are?

Just as too many Christians take the preacher's word, or the Sabbath School teacher's word for many theological items, too many gay Christians take the word of fellow Kinshippers and gay Christian leaders that the Bible doesn't really condemn homosexuality. But they themselves don't have the foundation to know what the Bible really says and what those clobber texts are really about. Many still have that bit of doubt in their minds that they could be wrong and that they really aren't "good enough" for God and for Heaven.

It isn't until one has studied and sought the answer for themselves and concluded that they really are 100% (not 99%) normal and OK just the way they are and that there is NO SIN and NO SECOND best about being gay, that they can be truly PROUD of who they are and then they can have GAY PRIDE.

Gay Pride is nothing more than unconditionally accepting yourself, and when you do that, you have no need for anyone else to accept you. You have the assurance that God accepts you not because you are gay or straight, good or bad, or any other adjective you can think of, but because Christ's blood covers you. PERIOD.

It has been a while since I've had the soapbox out to preach my sermons, so that was my sermonette for the day! <g>

Coming out was and is a long and many times difficult process, but on this side of the most troublesome parts of coming out and looking back, I am very happy to be gay and very proud of being gay. I wouldn't trade being gay for being straight for anything in the world. Being gay is FABULOUS! When it all boils down, being gay really isn't all that different from being straight, but I know God chose me to be gay in His plan of history and I feel it is an honor to understand that God KNEW I would be strong enough to handle it. I might be an inspiration to someone else struggling with the prejudices of society. I truly believe that although God loves ALL of His children, He loves His gay children just a bit more because of the extra struggle we have to deal with to stay close to Him in the religious communities we live in.

—November 17, 2003
Floyd Poenitz, SDA Kinship

About the Author

About the Authors

We are gay men and lesbians. We are bisexual, transgendered, and intersexed. We range in age from teenagers to senior citizens. We are of all ethnic and cultural diversities. We are short and tall, fat and skinny, energetic and sedentary. We are doctors, farmers, pastors, mothers and fathers, teachers, carpenters, musicians, counselors, librarians, nurses, computer experts, writers, managers, secretaries, engineers, mechanics, accountants, and unemployed.

Some of us are completely out and open, totally comfortable with ourselves and everyone else around us. Others of us are completely settled in our identity and our lives, but necessarily need to protect ourselves, our homes, and our jobs, and avoid exposure of others—parents, siblings, children, friends, and lovers. Still others of us are essentially closeted, but want and need to share our stories, even anonymously.

We are of many convictions and persuasions on issues of relationships, celibacy, the arts, religion, politics and activism within the gay community. Our sexual "preference" may be anywhere from promiscuity to lifelong monogamy to celibacy; but the sexual orientation we were born with is who we *are* and not what we *do*.

The one commonality we all share is our Seventh-day Adventist heritage. Regardless of our current church membership status, we were either born into the church, raised or significantly affected by Adventist parents or caregivers, or came into the church later in life.

And we are *not* heterosexual.